POEMS FOR REFUGEES

Pippa Haywood has worked as an actress in television and theatre for twenty years. She is best known for her role as Helen Brittas in *The Brittas Empire*. Her other work includes roles in *Dalziel and Pascoe*, *Office Gossip*, *Jonathan Creek*, *Holby City* and *The Inspector Lynley Mysteries*. Pippa has never compiled an anthology before, but felt inspired to do so by the events of September 11th and the Afghan War. She lives in South London with her family.

Pippa Haywood (ed.)

POEMS FOR REFUGEES

With a foreword by Martin Jarvis

VINTAGE

Published by Vintage 2002

2 4 6 8 10 9 7 5 3 1

Foreword copyright © Martin Jarvis 2002
Introduction copyright © Pippa Haywood 2002
For copyright of contributors see pp. 207–213

First published in Great Britain by Vintage 2002

Vintage
Random House, 20 Vauxhall Bridge Road,
London SW1V 2SA

Random House Australia (Pty) Limited
20 Alfred Street, Milsons Point, Sydney,
New South Wales 2061, Australia

Random House New Zealand Limited
18 Poland Road, Glenfield,
Auckland 10, New Zealand

Random House (Pty) Limited
Endulini, 5A Jubilee Road, Parktown 2193, South Africa

The Random House Group Limited Reg. No. 954009
www.randomhouse.co.uk

A CIP catalogue record for this book
is available from the British Library

ISBN 0 09 9287226

Typeset by Palimpsest Book Production Limited,
Polmont, Stirlingshire
Printed and bound in Great Britain by
Cox & Wyman Ltd, Reading, Berkshire

FOR ALL THE CHILDREN

CONTENTS

ON DIVERSITY

ON INNOCENCE AND EXPERIENCE

ON FAITH

ON PEACE

FOREWORD

We all remember where we were.

I was in Los Angeles, on the phone to Kate McCall, producer of BBC Radio Four's *Poetry Please*. It was early morning in California, mid-afternoon in England. As we talked, Kate mentioned she was just hearing from the next office that some sort of accident seemed to be happening, possibly a plane coming down. Somewhere. Maybe near New York. Ah well. We carried on talking, the project under discussion no doubt more important than the need for either of us to investigate whatever incident may (or may not) have occurred somewhere in America. Ten minutes or so later we finished our chat. I put the phone down and idly turned on the CNN news.

None of us will ever forget the horror of what we witnessed – unimaginable and yet we saw it – run and re-run across our screens. Attack on America. Attack on the world.

Now, thinking back, we hold in our hands this extraordinary collection of poetry. What I find completely remarkable about *Poems for Refugees* is the way in which the sensibilities of so many poets, past and present, can nail our own feelings. What a dazzling and necessary idea – a sublime mechanism to help focus our own thinking, our fear and anger, our sorrow and hope. A great hall of shining mirrors to reflect unnumbered aspects of the tragedy that has changed our world forever. In turning these pages, I find that favourite poems leap out at me in surprising ways. Through the prism of this anthology we make some amazing discoveries. Who would have thought, for instance, that Robert Burns' 'To a Mouse' (chosen by Seamus Heaney) beginning with the oh-so-familiar 'Wee, sleeket, cowran, tim'rous *beastie* . . .' could speak to us today of our fear of what lies ahead, beyond the uncertainty of the present. And I have never before appreciated the sense of triumph that exists in 'Fidele' from *Cymbeline*. Tony Robinson has shown me that my memory of it as a beautiful, if somewhat regretful dirge, is a distortion. Its final verse is a defiant fist-wave against the dying of the light.

The greatness of this poetry – to say nothing of the poets – provokes questions that we can't help asking ourselves: How did Matthew Arnold, say, or Sylvia Plath or W. B. Yeats know about September 11th? How did Rumi, a Persian poet writing in the thirteenth century, understand so well (in 'Only Breath') the knife-edge political issues we recognise now:

> There is a way between voice and presence
> where information flows.
> In disciplined silence it opens.
> With wandering talk it closes.

And, when we read Luis Enrique Mejía Godoy's 'Revenge', based on the words of Tomás Borge to his torturers, our brains boggle in wonderment at how such monumental compassion can endure. Godoy affirms that the only retaliation is forgiveness:

> My personal revenge
> Will be to give you these hands you once ill-treated
> With all their tenderness intact.

Poetry has the power to transcend time, to feed back to us a thousand visions of humanity. In writing of the past and the future, as well as the present, these poets speak to us for *all* time. Where, except in this collection, could we be privy to the twinned emotions of, say, Brecht and W. H. Auden (Brecht's 'Song from Mother Courage' translated by W. H. Auden) midwifed to our eyes (and ears) by the perception of Peter Hall's choice. How brilliant, too, that Adrian Mitchell ('William Blake Says: Everything That Lives is Holy') and John Keats ('To Autumn'), shaking hands across the centuries, can both, in different ways, celebrate the earth itself.

Comments that accompany many of the poems provide new insights. Sophie Thompson makes a superb point in explaining how 'A Drop of Unclouded Blood' by Brian Patten, which she has loved for a long time, returns to her, now, with fresh meaning. Looking again at my own choice of 'Colours' by Yevtushenko, more and more shades occur to me in the harsh light of current events.

A number of contributors suggest that we should try reading a chosen poem aloud. They're right and I would encourage you to give this a go. The *sound* of a poem invariably works alongside the text and extra resonances are likely to emerge. Buried ironies rise with unexpected force. Rhythms become clearer, often supplying further subliminal information to the ear and a fuller understanding. Plus, sometimes, a heart-stopping punch in the gut.

It's thrilling that this collection contains a clutch of outstanding new poems. 'The Voices Live' by Poet Laureate Andrew Motion is an affecting expression of how, in the aftermath, we must strive to remember the dead. He speaks specifically of September 11th but, along with poems written in other times about other places, it will undoubtedly live on. Similarly, in 'Grief', when Ben Okri speaks of 'those flaming towers' he is also reaching back and forward to embrace the world's suffering. Both poets indicate a chance of lessons learned from the tragedy. Andrew Motion shows us that the dead are 'the deep foundation of ourselves, our cornerstone'. Ben Okri urges us to use our grief to 'turn injustice into a flower'. In 'How shall we defeat The Enemy?' Michael Rosen pinpoints, with bitter humour, the moral confusion of many of us when he asks who, or what, actually is the enemy? And, in 'Spared', Wendy Cope re-runs on the screens of our memory the nightmare image of that couple, hand in hand, jumping from the tower:

> Spared all of this
> For now, how well I understand
> That love is all, is all there is.

Finally, I defy you not to be inspired by eight-year-old Cecily Haywood's 'Friends Across the World'. She reminds us, I believe, that we are all refugees, in one way or another. With simple blinding truth she demonstrates our need, never stronger than now, to give – and to accept – unconditional love.

So try to keep your hopes up
When you are feeling down
Because you know that friends like me
Will love you all year round.

Let's keep saying that – aloud.

Martin Jarvis
London
January 2002

I started working on this project shortly after September 11th when the west started lurching toward its seemingly inevitable 'war against terrorism'. I sat and watched with growing concern as images of a country, already devastated by twenty years and more of war and famine, was drawn into the sights of the world's greatest military power.

One evening in particular I was watching TV whilst my happy, healthy two-year-old bounded around in front of the screen. I saw two tiny Afghan children, about the same age as my own, scratching in the dust bowl that appeared to be their home. They were looking for stores of grain that rats had buried that they could steal to eat. This was their 'play'. It was also their existence. The contrast was stark and pitiful. I had to try to do something.

The idea that came to me later that night was to ask well-known people to suggest poems that could be sold as an anthology in aid of the humanitarian relief effort; a sort of 'poem aid' or 'poetic relief'.

I contacted the few friends who I thought would be well-known enough to draw in others through an appeal letter and then set about the task of asking a star-studded list if they would like to contribute. I had no idea what to expect – it could have fizzled out in a couple of weeks with people just ignoring my request; they might find it an intrusion, yet another demand on their time. The response came as a flood of enthusiastic, heartfelt suggestions and I found that my efforts were reaping unexpected rewards.

I hadn't anticipated the joy at discovering new (to me) poems and poets, the thrill of telephone conversations with the likes of Geoffrey Palmer, Lindsay Duncan, Martin Jarvis and Mike Leigh – people whose work I have long enjoyed and admired – the barely disguised near swooning as I listened to the velvet tones of Ben Okri, dictating his new work specially written in response to the situation, over the phone to me. Then there were the connections between the contributors themselves. Will Wain, the son of John Wain whose poem Judi Dench had chosen, was delighted that his father's poem was one of Dame Judi's favourites, John Hegley found that he had a fan in Richard

Wilson; Seamus Heaney was 'glad indeed' that Jon Snow had chosen his Chorus from *The Cure at Troy*, and Jon Snow was 'extremely chuffed' that Seamus Heaney had been so pleased. It was hugely gratifying to act as a catalyst to bring all these fine people together and to witness this growing thread linking them all together.

Then there were the poems themselves. I'm no poetry expert. In fact it still surprises me that I thought of poetry as a way of raising money in the first place. But there was an intuitive need to explore the written word further. The language of the news reports spoke of the facts and figures, the horrors and the devastation, but they couldn't go further, they couldn't touch the soul. As the poems came in some made me cry: some speak with such clarity about themes I struggle to articulate, some allow one to escape into a place of beauty and stillness, others force you to confront the very heart of the problem, but all do so through connecting with the reader at a deeper level. The poems have made me full of wonder at the ability of the creative word to transform our confused state of mind and to give it clarity and meaning.

So these were the thrills. Then there was the hard work. The people I was trying to contact are not the sort of people you find in the phone book. Sometimes you pretty well need to hire a private detective just to get a forwarding address! Some poetry suggestions came in as just titles on pieces of paper until I had searched them out. I spent many hours looking for a poet called Later Svendborg. I had the entire Poetry Library searching for him on their websites. It was only when another contributor suggested a Brecht poem that I discovered that this was a chapter heading in his *Poems 1913–1956* and that Svendborg was where he had written these particular works. Later. Then there were permissions to ask for on any poems written by living poets or those who had died less than 70 years ago. Another trip to the Poetry Library, this time to find out when Rumi had lived. I had no idea. His work seemed modern and yet timeless. I had several contributors suggesting his work and knowing that he had written in Afghanistan I thought seeking permission could take ages. I waited as the librarian went to find out, feeling rather badly that I was hoping this man was dead and more than 70 years dead if possible! She came back saying, 'Well I think you should be OK, he died in 1273.' Relief. 'Of course you'll still need to seek permission from the translators.' Stifled moan.

There was also the small point of finding someone to publish the collection. What on earth was I going to do with this extraordinary list of people and poems if I couldn't find anyone to take it into print? Many of the actors had said what a good idea it would be to do a mass reading, or an audio tape – at one stage I thought it might be just Bill Nighy and me standing on a street corner, cap at foot and poetry book in hand, offering our small voices to the wind! However Vintage at Random House to their great credit saved us from that fate and took the project on. And there will, indeed, be an accompanying audio tape produced by CSA Telltapes.

It has been fascinating seeing which poems have been chosen by which personalities. Sometimes the person and the choice seem synonymous. Pablo Neruda's 'Your Laughter' could only have been chosen by Martin Clunes, and I could imagine Virginia McKenna speaking to me directly when I read her choice of Brian Patten's wise and beautiful 'A blade of grass'.

I hope the enjoyment of the poems will be enhanced by the inclusion of the accompanying statements which some of the contributors offered. I think these few words give an insight into the personality of the contributor, and some reveal touching stories about why they made their choice. Where it just states that a poem has been chosen by the contributor it is because they preferred their chosen poem to speak for itself.

I have tried to group the poems under headings which reveal the area the contributor has turned to in response to the situation; a straight look at war, the plight of the refugee, a hope of transformation, love, faith, or a need for stillness and peace.

Included in this collection are a number of works that have been written in response to September 11th and the ensuing situation. These come from Wendy Cope, Tony Harrison, Andrew Motion, Ben Okri, Adrian Mitchell, Michael Rosen and Andrew Darnton, and in my opinion are some of the most heartfelt and inspiring pieces in the whole collection. These poems are followed by the year in which they were written. Where a poem does not state that it was 'chosen' it was either requested by me or offered as the author's own contribution.

There are also two pieces written by children. I asked a few individuals and a local school if they would like to consider offering something. I asked them to try to imagine what it might feel like to be a refugee and what they might want to say or offer to a refugee child if they had the opportunity to do so. The results were touching and clear. They were so transparently outraged. This is wrong. I wish I could help them. I wish I could stop it. I hope that these two shining examples will serve to represent this generation's feelings.

The last but nonetheless very important task was to choose which charity should benefit from the proceeds of the book. I wanted to choose a group that were supplying essential food and equipment to the refugee camps, trying to get supplies into the regions of Afghanistan most at risk from famine and of being cut off during the winter months, and who were thinking ahead to the sorts of development work which will put the country and its citizens back on their feet once the initial basic needs have been met. There are thankfully very many charities engaged in all these areas and carrying out life-saving work in the most impossible situations of negligible security and safety. I also wanted it to be a charity which focused on children as it had been through children that the project had been inspired in the first place. I finally settled on War Child. They have been extremely helpful and supportive of the project and I felt that they were involved in all the areas of relief work that I wanted the proceeds from the book to be supporting. At a refugee camp in Herāt they have set up a bakery similar to the ones they pioneered in Kosovo during the Balkan crisis, which will feed 25,000 people a day. They have already helped Acted, the French relief agency, to get some of the essential wheatflour into north-east Afghanistan and have plans drawn up to help create mine-free safe playgrounds for the children once the basic-needs work has been achieved. I know that they will put the proceeds from this book to excellent use.

Through my contact with so many people during this project I feel that I have touched a common chord. No matter what we feel about the political action being taken in the so-called 'war against terrorism' there is a heartfelt and universally shared sympathy for the ordinary citizens of Afghanistan who have suffered living in a poverty-stricken, war-torn country under a brutal regime for too long. There have been many grand statements saying that this time when the west moves out its military force, Afghanistan will not be forgotten. So whenever you pick up this book and read a poem or two, cast a glance in that direction and see if we are holding fast to those promises.

Pippa Haywood
London
January 2002

on September 11th

SPARED

It wasn't you, it wasn't me,
Up there, two thousand feet above
A New York street. We're safe, and free,
A little while, to live and love,

Imagining what might have been –
The phone-call from the blazing tower,
A last farewell on the machine,
While someone sleeps another hour,

Or worse, perhaps, to say goodbye
And listen to each other's pain,
Send helpless love across the sky,
Knowing we'll never meet again,

Or jump together, hand in hand,
To certain death. Spared all of this
For now, how well I understand
That love is all, is all there is.

                              Wendy Cope, 2001

SEPTEMBER 1, 1939

I sit in one of the dives
On Fifty-Second Street
Uncertain and afraid
As the clever hopes expire
Of a low dishonest decade:
Waves of anger and fear
Circulate over the bright
And darkened lands of the earth,
Obsessing our private lives;
The unmentionable odour of death
Offends the September night.

Accurate scholarship can
Unearth the whole offence
From Luther until now
That has driven a culture mad,
Find what occurred at Linz,
What huge imago made
A psychopathic god:
I and the public know
What all schoolchildren learn,
Those to whom evil is done
Do evil in return.

Exiled Thucydides knew
All that a speech can say
About Democracy,
And what dictators do,
The elderly rubbish they talk
To an apathetic grave;
Analysed all in his book,
The enlightenment driven away,
The habit-forming pain,

Mismanagement and grief:
We must suffer them all again.

Into this neutral air
Where blind skyscrapers use
Their full height to proclaim
The strength of Collective Man,
Each language pours its vain
Competitive excuse:
But who can live for long
In an euphoric dream;
Out of the mirror they stare,
Imperialism's face
And the international wrong.

Faces along the bar
Cling to their average day:
The lights must never go out,
The music must always play,
All the conventions conspire
To make this fort assume
The furniture of home;
Lest we should see where we are,
Lost in a haunted wood,
Children afraid of the night
Who have never been happy or good.

The windiest militant trash
Important Persons shout
Is not so crude as our wish:
What mad Nijinsky wrote
About Diaghilev
Is true of the normal heart;
For the error bred in the bone
Of each woman and each man

Craves what it cannot have,
Not universal love
But to be loved alone.

From the conservative dark
Into the ethical life
The dense commuters come,
Repeating their morning vow,
'I *will* be true to the wife,
'I'll concentrate more on my work',
And helpless governors wake
To resume their compulsory game:
Who can release them now,
Who can reach the deaf,
Who can speak for the dumb?

All I have is a voice
To undo the folded lie,
The romantic lie in the brain
Of the sensual man-in-the-street
And the lie of Authority
Whose buildings grope the sky:
There is no such thing as the State
And no one exists alone;
Hunger allows no choice
To the citizen or the police;
We must love one another or die.

Defenceless under the night
Our world in stupor lies;
Yet, dotted everywhere,
Ironic points of light
Flash out wherever the Just
Exchange their messages:
May I, composed like them

Of Eros and of dust,
Beleaguered by the same
Negation and despair,
Show an affirming flame.

W. H. Auden (1907–73)

Chosen by Stephen Fry

I was asked if I might think of a poem for this collection just a week or so after the attack on the World Trade Centre in September 2001. Auden's 'September 1, 1939' struck me as blisteringly and almost appallingly appropriate. Set in New York, and contemplating a world erupting into violence, tyranny and hatred, it does what poetry does supremely – it takes huge abstract and geopolitical ideas and makes them personal, internal and human. It all comes down, after all, to love. He seems to be at the height of his poetic powers here, using a language of enormous authority and confidence. His phrase 'low dishonest decade' has stuck to the thirties like 'roaring' to the twenties. There's a story that in later years he wanted to change the last line of the penultimate stanza to 'We must love one another and die', having turned into something of a grouchy pedant in later years. 'We're going to die anyway,' he would remark testily. 'So the line doesn't make sense.' It does of course, it makes terrific sense. Fortunately all editions stick to the original version.

THE NEWS-REEL

Since Munich, what? A tangle of black film
Squirming like bait upon the floor of my mind
And scissors clicking daily. I am inclined
To pick these pictures now but will hold back
Till memory has elicited from this blind
Drama its threads of vision, the intrusions
Of value upon fact, that sudden unconfined
Wind of understanding that blew out
From people's hands and faces, undesigned
Evidence of design, that change of climate
Which did not last but happens often enough
To give us hope that fact is a facade
And that there is an organism behind
Its brittle littleness, a rhythm and a meaning,
Something half-conjectured and half-divined,
Something to give way to and so find.

Louis MacNeice (1907–63)

Chosen by Nick Hornby

I think anyone who felt or perhaps still feels confused about September 11th
will recognise the impulse that must have led MacNeice to his poem, written
in 1942, especially as we now have such a bigger and messier tangle of black
film to contend with.

IN TIME OF 'THE BREAKING OF NATIONS'

I

Only a man harrowing clods
   In a slow silent walk
With an old horse that stumbles and nods
   Half asleep as they stalk.

II

Only thin smoke without flame
   From the heaps of couch-grass;
Yet this will go onward the same
   Though Dynasties pass.

III

Yonder a maid and her wight
   Come whispering by:
War's annals will cloud into night
   Ere their story die.

Thomas Hardy (1840–1928)

Chosen by Douglas Hodge

September 11th – as it's now called – found me scanning my poetry books for some solace. This poem by Thomas Hardy straightaway came to mind – maybe some comfort – as one of the great hinges of human history creaked open and all sides seemed ready to let slip all the bile of war . . .

MUSÉE DES BEAUX ARTS

About suffering they were never wrong,
The Old Masters; how well they understood
Its human position; how it takes place
While someone else is eating or opening a window or just walking
    dully along;
How, when the aged are reverently, passionately waiting
For the miraculous birth, there always must be
Children who did not specially want it to happen, skating
On a pond at the edge of the wood:
They never forgot
That even the dreadful martyrdom must run its course
Anyhow in a corner, some untidy spot
Where the dogs go on with their doggy life and the torturer's horse
Scratches its innocent behind on a tree.

In Breughel's *Icarus*, for instance: how everything turns away
Quite leisurely from the disaster; the ploughman may
Have heard the splash, the forsaken cry,
But for him it was not an important failure; the sun shone
As it had to on the white legs disappearing into the green
Water; and the expensive delicate ship that must have seen
Something amazing, a boy falling out of the sky,
Had somewhere to get to and sailed calmly on.

W. H. Auden (1907–73)

Chosen by Lindsay Duncan and by Stephen Daldry

on war

WAR

war, war, war,
the yellow monster,
the eater of mind
and body.
war,
the indescribable,
the pleasure of
the mad,
the final argument
of
ungrown men.

does it belong?

do we?

as we approach
the last flash of
our chance.

one flower left.

one second.

breathing like this.

Charles Bukowski (1920–94)

Chosen by Mike Leigh

Wry, dry, simple, specific, moving.

HOW SHALL WE DEFEAT THE ENEMY?

How shall we defeat The Enemy?

We shall defeat The Enemy by making alliances.

Who shall we make alliances with?

With people in whose interests it is, to be enemies with The
    Enemy.

How shall we win an alliance with these people?

We shall win an alliance with these people by giving them money
    and arms.

And after that?

They will help us defeat The Enemy.

Has The Enemy got money and arms?

Yes.

How did The Enemy get money and arms?

He was once someone in whose interests it was, to be enemies with
    our enemy.

Which enemy was this?

Someone in whose interest it had once been, to be enemies with
    an enemy.

Michael Rosen, 2001

WHEN STATESMEN GRAVELY SAY

When Statesmen gravely say 'We must be realistic',
The chances are they're weak and, therefore, pacifistic,
But when they speak of Principles, look out: perhaps
Their generals are already poring over maps.

W. H. Auden (1907–73)

Chosen by Robert Powell

It seems as apt now as when it was written. Maybe more so.

EPITAPH ON A TYRANT

Perfection, of a kind, was what he was after,
And the poetry he invented was easy to understand;
He knew human folly like the back of his hand,
And was greatly interested in armies and fleets;
When he laughed, respectable senators burst with laughter,
And when he cried the little children died in the streets.

W. H. Auden (1907–73)

Chosen by John Sessions

I chose this poem because it is short and to the point and says everything it has to say.

THE SECOND COMING

Turning and turning in the widening gyre
The falcon cannot hear the falconer;
Things fall apart; the centre cannot hold;
Mere anarchy is loosed upon the world,
The blood-dimmed tide is loosed, and everywhere
The ceremony of innocence is drowned;
The best lack all conviction, while the worst
Are full of passionate intensity.

Surely some revelation is at hand;
Surely the Second Coming is at hand.
The Second Coming! Hardly are those words out
When a vast image out of *Spiritus Mundi*
Troubles my sight: somewhere in sands of the desert
A shape with lion body and the head of a man,
A gaze blank and pitiless as the sun,
Is moving its slow thighs, while all about it
Reel shadows of the indignant desert birds.
The darkness drops again; but now I know
That twenty centuries of stony sleep
Were vexed to nightmare by a rocking cradle,
And what rough beast, its hour come round at last,
Slouches towards Bethlehem to be born?

William Butler Yeats (1865–1939)

Chosen by Anna Massey

The images that this poem evoke seem to me peculiarly and mysteriously
relevant to the events that are unfolding in these troubled times.

WAITING FOR THE BARBARIANS

What are we waiting for, assembled in the forum?

    The barbarians are due here today.

Why isn't anything going on in the senate?
Why are the senators sitting there without legislating?

    Because the barbarians are coming today.
    What's the point of senators making laws now?
    Once the barbarians are here, they'll do the legislating.

Why did our emperor get up so early,
and why is he sitting enthroned at the city's main gate,
in state, wearing the crown?

    Because the barbarians are coming today
    and the emperor's waiting to receive their leader.
    He's even got a scroll to give him,
    loaded with titles, with imposing names.

Why have our two consuls and praetors come out today
wearing their embroidered, their scarlet togas?
Why have they put on bracelets with so many amethysts,
rings sparkling with magnificent emeralds?
Why are they carrying elegant canes
beautifully worked in silver and gold?

    Because the barbarians are coming today
    and things like that dazzle the barbarians.

Why don't our distinguished orators turn up as usual
to make their speeches, say what they have to say?

Because the barbarians are coming today
and they're bored by rhetoric and public speaking.

Why this sudden bewilderment, this confusion?
(How serious people's faces have become.)
Why are the streets and squares emptying so rapidly,
everyone going home lost in thought?

Because night has fallen and the barbarians haven't come.
And some of our men just in from the border say
there are no barbarians any longer.

Now what's going to happen to us without barbarians?
Those people were a kind of solution.

C. P. Cavafy (1863–1933); translated by Edmund Keeley
and Philip Sherrard

Chosen by John Fortune

THE BALLAD OF THE SHRIEKING MAN

A shrieking man stood in the square
And he harangued the smart café
In which a bowlered codger sat
A-twirling of a fine moustache
A-drinking of a fine Tokay

And it was Monday and the town
Was working in a kind of peace
Excepting where the shrieking man
A-waving of his tattered limbs
Glared at the codger's trouser-crease

Saying

Coffee's mad
And tea is mad
And so are gums and teeth and lips.
The horror ships that ply the seas
The horror tongues that plough the teeth
The coat
The tie
The trouser clips
The purple sergeant with the bugger-grips
Will string you up with all their art
And laugh their socks off as you blow apart.

The codger seeming not to hear
Winked at the waiter, paid the bill
And walked the main street out of town
Beyond the school, beyond the works
Where the shrieking man pursued him still
And there the town beneath them lay

And there the desperate river ran.
The codger smiled a purple smile.
A finger sliced his waistcoat ope
And he rounded on the shrieking man

Saying

Tramps are mad
And truth is mad
And so are trees and trunks and tracks.
The horror maps have played us true.
The horror moon that slits the clouds
The gun
The goon
The burlap sacks
The purple waistcoats of the natterjacks
Have done their bit as you can see
To prise the madness from our sanity.

On Wednesday when the day was young
Two shrieking men came into town
And stopped before the smart café
In which another codger sat
Twirling his whiskers with a frown

And as they shrieked and slapped their knees
The codger's toes began to prance
Within the stitching of their caps
Which opened like a set of jaws
And forced him out to join the dance

Saying

Arms are mad
And legs are mad

27

And all the spaces in between.
The horror spleen that bursts its sack
The horror purple as it lunges through
The lung
The bung
The jumping-bean
The I-think-you-know-what-you-think-I-mean
Are up in arms against the state
And all the body will disintegrate.

On Saturday the town was full
As people strolled in seeming peace
Until three shrieking men appeared
And danced before the smart café
And laughed and jeered and slapped their knees

And there a hundred codgers sat.
A hundred adam's apples rose
And rubbed against their collar studs
Until the music came in thuds
And all the men were on their toes

Saying

Hearts are mad
And minds are mad
And bats are moons and moons are bats.
The horror cats that leap the tiles
The horror slates that catch the wind
The lice
The meat
The burning ghats
The children buried in the butter vats
The steeple crashing through the bedroom roof
Will be your answer if you need a proof.

The codgers poured into the square
And soon their song was on all lips
And all did dance and slap their knees
Until a horseman came in view –
The sergeant with the bugger-grips!

He drew his cutlass, held it high
And brought it down on hand and head
And ears were lopped and limbs were chopped
And still the sergeant slashed and slew
Until the codger crew lay dead

Saying

God is mad
And I am mad
And I am God and you are me.
The horror peace that boils the sight
The horror God turning out the light.
The Christ
Who killed
The medlar tree
Is planning much the same for you and me
And here's a taste of what's in store –
Come back again if you should want some more.

On Sunday as they hosed the streets
I went as usual to pray
And cooled my fingers at the stoup
And when the wafer touched my tongue
I thought about that fine Tokay

And so I crossed the empty square
And met the waiter with a wink
A-sweeping up of severed heads

29

A-piling up of bowler hats
And he muttered as he poured my drink

Saying

Waiting's mad
And stating's mad
And understating's mad as hell.
The undertakings we have made
The wonder breaking from the sky
The pin
The pen
The poisoned well
The purple sergeant with the nitrate smell
Have won their way and while we wait
The horror ships have passed the straits —
The vice
The vine
The strangler fig
The fault of thinking small and acting big
Have primed the bomb and pulled the pin
And we're all together when the roof falls in!

James Fenton (1949–)

Chosen by Ian McEwan

PARENTAGE

*'When Augustus Caesar legislated against the unmarried citizens of Rome,
he declared them to be, in some sort, the slayers of the people.'*

Ah no! not these!
These, who were childless, are not they who gave
So many dead unto the journeying wave,
The helpless nurslings of the cradling seas;
Not they who doomed by infallible decrees
Unnumbered man to the innumerable grave.

But those who slay
Are fathers. Theirs are armies. Death is theirs –
The death of innocences and despairs;
The dying of the golden and the grey.
The sentence, when these speak it, has no Nay.
And she who slays is she who bears, who bears.

Alice Meynell (1847–1922)

Chosen by Germaine Greer

'SONG' *FROM* MOTHER COURAGE

When courage fades, when hopes are fading,
Think on the victory ahead,
For War is but a kind of trading:
Instead of cheese, it deals in lead.

Some have done deeds they took a pride in,
Some slyly sought their lives to save:
With care they dug a hole to hide in,
But merely dug an early grave.

How many brave fire, hail and thunder
In hope to reach a quiet shore,
Who, when they get there, only wonder
Exactly what they braved them for.

Bertolt Brecht (1898–1956); translated by W. H. Auden

Chosen by Peter Hall

SPECIES BARRIER

An Afghan mega food-Aid drop
this plump cow banquet but no parachute,
not carved up into packs of steak and chop,
or some collaterally slaughtered brute?
Or is it a whole cow colony of spores
with no rushed R & D to 'weaponise',
an FMD carcass with raw sores,
the staggers stampeding from the skies?
Not Aid-drop mega-feast, not germ warfare
though it's pregnant with explosive, putrid gas,
this maggot Mecca crescendoing with prayer
will never feed the hungry folk who pass.
An Afghan's total herd like some gunned stray
from culled Cumbria dumped on Kabul,
the colluding cabinet of the hooked UK
still committing its 'contiguous cull'.

Tony Harrison, 2001

CARRION COMFORT

Not, I'll not, carrion comfort, Despair, not feast on thee;
Not untwist — slack they may be — these last strands of man
In me or, most weary, cry *I can no more*. I can;
Can something, hope, wish day come, not choose not to be.
But ah, but O thou terrible, why wouldst thou rude on me
Thy wring-world right foot rock? lay a lionlimb against me? scan
With darksome devouring eyes my bruisèd bones? and fan,
O in turns of tempest, me heaped there; me frantic to avoid thee
    and flee?

Why? That my chaff might fly; my grain lie, sheer and clear.
Nay in all that toil, that coil, since (seems) I kissed the rod,
Hand rather, my heart lo! lapped strength, stole joy, would
    laugh, cheer.
Cheer whom though? The hero whose heaven-handling flung me,
    foot trod
Me? Or me that fought him? O which one? is it each one? That
    night, that year
Of now done darkness I wretch lay wrestling with (my God!)
    my God.

Gerard Manley Hopkins (1844–89)

Chosen by Jane Horrocks and Nick Vivian

DULCE ET DECORUM EST

Bent double, like old beggars under sacks,
Knock-kneed, coughing like hags, we cursed through sludge,
Till on the haunting flares we turned our backs
And towards our distant rest began to trudge.
Men marched asleep. Many had lost their boots
But limped on, blood-shod. All went lame; all blind;
Drunk with fatigue; deaf even to the hoots
Of tired, outstripped Five-Nines that dropped behind.

Gas! Gas! Quick, boys! – An ecstasy of fumbling,
Fitting the clumsy helmets just in time;
But someone still was yelling out and stumbling
And flound'ring like a man in fire or lime . . .
Dim, through the misty panes and thick green light,
As under a green sea, I saw him drowning.

In all my dreams, before my helpless sight,
He plunges at me, guttering, choking, drowning.

If in some smothering dreams you too could pace
Behind the wagon that we flung him in,
And watch the white eyes writhing in his face,
His hanging face, like a devil's sick of sin;
If you could hear, at every jolt, the blood
Come gargling from the froth-corrupted lungs,
Obscene as cancer, bitter as the cud
Of vile, incurable sores on innocent tongues, –
My friend, you would not tell with such high zest
To children ardent for some desperate glory,
The old Lie: Dulce et decorum est
Pro patria mori.

Wilfred Owen (1893–1918)

Chosen by John Thaw and Sheila Hancock

In an age of 'smart bombs' and supposed avoidance of 'collateral damage', it is wise to remind ourselves that the reality of war is still obscene.

MOTTO

In the dark times
Will there also be singing?
Yes, there will also be singing
About the dark times.

Bertolt Brecht (1898–1956); translated by John Willett

Chosen by Caryl Churchill

PERSONAL END OF A WAR

I think my brain stopped when I read the words
because there was nothing in my head –
nothing –
and you know my thoughts
have always been like birds in an aviary
flying all ways in color;
it had all closed down to a gray silence.
Then you took the letter from me
and touched my arm
and a Roman candle went up inside me
and I remembered from the beginning:
a fat baby
a happy boy
a young man like you, young again,
a young man with a heart like a sounding guitar.

They said he was a hero.
Do you think a hero in the family
is better than a living son?

Margaret Flanagan Eicher

Chosen by Louise Jameson

I found this poem many years ago in an anthology of Women's Work on
Peace and War, called *My Country is the Whole World*. It isn't hugely hopeful
but it does pose an extremely thought-provoking question for every parent.
I think this anthology a truly lovely idea, if only to keep these atrocities in
the forefront of our minds, thereby preventing repetition.

THE END OF THE WAR

The end of the war. I took it quietly
Enough. I tried to wash the dirt out of
My hair and from under my fingernails,
I dressed in clean white clothes and went to bed.
I heard the dust falling between the walls.

Howard Nemerov (1920–91)

Chosen by Richard Eyre

THE SURVIVOR

I am twenty-four
led to slaughter
I survived.

The following are empty synonyms:
man and beast
love and hate
friend and foe
darkness and light.

The way of killing men and beasts is the same
I've seen it:
truckfuls of chopped-up men
who will not be saved.

Ideas are mere words:
virtue and crime
truth and lies
beauty and ugliness
courage and cowardice.

Virtue and crime weigh the same
I've seen it:
in a man who was both
criminal and virtuous.

I seek a teacher and a master
may he restore my sight hearing and speech
may he again name objects and ideas
may he separate darkness from light.

I am twenty-four
led to slaughter
I survived.

Tadeusz Rozewicz (1921–);
translated by Adam Czerniawski

Chosen by Andrew Motion

This brilliant, brilliantly-translated poem succeeds by seeming to take the simplest and most direct route to its subject. Yet its plainness contains complex balances and reconciliations – between abstraction and physical reality, between a moral life and a circumstantial existence, between resilience and despair. It is unforgettable, shocking, and unignorably consoling.

AT WAR

Hatred
Hatred is everywhere
War is agonising
Don't you dare
Old men argue while young men die

Disaster and pain
Caused by your shame

We are all innocent, no one to blame

I hear you cry . . .
children with no home
forever left to roam

Mothers screaming
a child in pain

Mothers numb
trouble in their way

Hospitals full to the brim

I am only a child
I know that this is wrong
So much hatred you feel inside

Listen to my song
Listen
Listen
Listen

Before the world is gone!

*Kellie Griffith, Yacoub Didi, Joanne Daniels,
Mark Russell and Daniel Lewis, aged ten*

on death and dying
and our ancestors

THE VOICES LIVE

The voices live which are the voices lost:
we hear them and we answer, or we try
but words are nervous when we need them most
and stammer, stop, or dully slide away

so everything they mean to summon up
is always just too far, just out of reach,
unless our memories give time the slip
and learn the lesson that heart-wisdoms teach

of how in grief we find a way to keep
the dead beside us as our time goes on –
invisible and silent but the deep
foundation of ourselves, our cornerstone.

Andrew Motion, 2001

DEFYING GRAVITY

Gravity is one of the oldest tricks in the book.
Let go of the book and it abseils to the ground
As if, at the centre of the earth, spins a giant yo-yo
To which everything is attached by an invisible string.

Tear out a page of the book and make an aeroplane.
Launch it. For an instant it seems that you have fashioned
A shape that can outwit air, that has slipped the knot.
But no. The earth turns, the winch tightens, it is wound in.

One of my closest friends is, at the time of writing,
Attempting to defy gravity, and will surely succeed.
Eighteen months ago he was playing rugby,
Now, seven stones lighter, his wife carries him aw –

Kwardly from room to room. Arranges him gently
Upon the sofa for the visitors. 'How are things?'
Asks one, not wanting to know. Pause. 'Not too bad.'
(Open brackets. Condition inoperable. Close brackets.)

Soon now, the man that I love (not the armful of bones)
Will defy gravity. Freeing himself from the tackle
He will sidestep the opposition and streak down the wing
Towards a dimension as yet unimagined.

Back where the strings are attached there will be a service
And homage paid to the giant yo-yo. A box of left-overs
Will be lowered into a space on loan from the clay.
Then, weighted down, the living will walk wearily away.

Roger McGough (1937–)

A CLEAR DAY AND NO MEMORIES

No soldiers in the scenery,
No thoughts of people now dead,
As they were fifty years ago:
Young and living in a live air,
Young and walking in the sunshine,
Bending in blue dresses to touch something –
Today the mind is not part of the weather.

Today the air is clear of everything.
It has no knowledge except of nothingness
And it flows over us without meanings,
As if none of us had ever been here before
And are not now: in this shallow spectacle,
This invisible activity, this sense.

Wallace Stevens (1879–1955)

Chosen by John Bird

This poem was written not long before Stevens died, in 1955: it is not so much about death as a preparation for it, and a rather triumphant assertion of what he called the 'exactest poverty' of language in the midst of the unthinking affluence of life. What I like about it is its absolute toughness combined with a kind of unflinching gaiety.

THE DEPARTURE LOUNGE

'He's gone to the departure lounge,' you said –
Meaning, of course, he had not long to live.
Your tone was serious. I smiled instead,
Struck by the metaphor you chose to give
The irreversible process of decline
In one you must have loved (in your own way),
And how a quirk of speech can redefine
The real sense of loss.
              Now, every day,
The faces have grown thinner round the bar.
We lose each other and we have not met –
Our separation ever more bizarre,
Based as it is on mutual regret,
Ironic in its total unity.
Death and the fear of death, of sensual fraud,
Darken the private chambers of the city
That echoes, like a vast communal ward,
With a dry-throated rage.
              Clenching our pills
We leave our doctors, newly diagnosed,
Think only of the virus that it kills
And how much to confide – or are composed.
Armed with a clearer knowledge as we chance
The cool controlled reaction: I recall
Profound relief, a kind of arrogance.
I had not reckoned that the sky would fall.

Adam Johnson (1965–93)

Chosen by Christina Gorna

By the time Adam Johnson died of AIDS at the age of twenty-eight, he had published three collections of poetry. 'The Departure Lounge' typifies his spirit of bravery and hope. His poems are an inspiration; strangely they never fail to cheer me up. It was said of Adam that all his friends thought that they were his *best* friend. I was proud to be one of them and to be able to share the legacy of his astonishingly mature and sensitive work with the readers of this anthology.

GROWING OLDER

I want the mornings to last longer
   And the twilight to linger.
I want to clutch the present to my bosom
   And never let it go.
I resent the tyranny of the clock on the wall,
   Nagging me to get on with my day.
I am a time traveller,
   But a traveller who would rather walk than fly
And yet it's joyous growing older,
   The major battles of life are over.
There is an armistice of the heart
   And a truce is signed with passion.
To forgive becomes easier
   And reason takes the place of strife.
There's one more hurdle left for crossing
   Though you're reluctant to approach it.
If you have lived your life with love
   There will be nothing at all to fear,
Because a warm welcome awaits you on the other side.

Sir Harry Secombe (1921–2001)

Chosen by June Whitfield

This poem written by Harry Secombe was read at his memorial service in Westminster Abbey by Bill Cotton. Harry was loved and respected by all who knew him.

SNOW

In the gloom of whiteness,
In the great silence of snow,
A child was sighing
And bitterly saying: 'Oh,
They have killed a white bird up there on her nest,
The down is fluttering from her breast!'
And still it fell through that dusky brightness
On the child crying for the bird of the snow.

Edward Thomas (1878–1917)

Chosen by Sarah Lawson

I chose this poem because it was so evocative of the sadness of the Afghan orphans. A lovely bird shot. Another death in an awful war.

THE LONESOME DEATH
OF HATTIE CARROLL

William Zanzinger killed poor Hattie Carroll
With a cane that he twirled around his diamond ring finger
At a Baltimore hotel society gath'rin'.
And the cops were called in and his weapon took from him
As they rode him in custody down to the station
And booked William Zanzinger for first-degree murder.
But you who philosophize disgrace and criticize all fears,
Take the rag away from your face.
Now ain't the time for your tears.

William Zanzinger, who at twenty-four years
Owns a tobacco farm of six hundred acres
With rich wealthy parents who provide and protect him
And high office relations in the politics of Maryland,
Reacted to his deed with a shrug of his shoulders
And swear words and sneering, and his tongue it was snarling,
In a matter of minutes on bail was out walking.
But you who philosophize disgrace and criticize all fears,
Take the rag away from your face.
Now ain't the time for your tears.

Hattie Carroll was a maid of the kitchen.
She was fifty-one years old and gave birth to ten children
Who carried the dishes and took out the garbage
And never sat once at the head of the table
And didn't even talk to the people at the table
Who just cleaned up all the food from the table
And emptied the ashtrays on a whole other level,
Got killed by a blow, lay slain by a cane
That sailed through the air and came down through the room,
Doomed and determined to destroy all the gentle.
And she never done nothing to William Zanzinger.

But you who philosophize disgrace and criticize all fears,
Take the rag away from your face.
Now ain't the time for your tears.

In the courtroom of honor, the judge pounded his gavel
To show that all's equal and that the courts are on the level
And that the strings in the books ain't pulled and persuaded
And that even the nobles get properly handled
Once that the cops have chased after and caught 'em
And that the ladder of law has no top and no bottom,
Stared at the person who killed for no reason
Who just happened to be feelin' that way without warnin'.
And he spoke through his cloak, most deep and distinguished,
And handed out strongly, for penalty and repentance,
William Zanzinger with a six-month sentence.
Oh, but you who philosophize disgrace and criticize all fears,
Bury the rag deep in your face
For now's the time for your tears.

Bob Dylan (1941–)

Chosen by Sue Johnston

THE ONE MINUTES OF SILENCE

I have stood for so many minutes of silence in my time.
I have stood many one minutes for
Blair Peach,
Colin Roach
And
Akhtar Ali Baig,
And every time I stand for them
The silence kills me.
I have performed on stage for
Alton Manning
Now I stand in silence for
Alton Manning,
One minute at a time, and every minute counts.
When I am standing still in the still silence
I always wonder if there is something
About the deaths of
Marcia Laws
Oscar Okoye
Or
Joy Gardner
That can wake dis sleepy nation.
Are they too hot for cool Britannia?

When I stand in silence for
Michael Menson
Manish Patel
Or
Ricky Reel
I am overwhelmed with honest militancy,
I've listened to the life stories of
Stephen Lawrence

Kenneth Severin
And
Shiji Lapite

And now I hear them crying for all of us,
I hear so much when I stand
For a minute of silence.

The truth is,
Being the person that I am
I would rather shout for hours,
I wanna make a big noise for my sisters,
Mothers and brothers,
I want to bear a million love children
To overrun the culture of cruelty,
I want babies that will live for a lifetime,
I don't want to silence their souls
I don't want them to be seen and not heard,
I want them to be heard
I want them loud and proud.

My athletic feet are tired
Of standing for one minutes of silence for
Christopher Alder,
I should be dancing with him;
Ricky Reel
Stephen Lawrence
And
Brian Douglas
Make silence very difficult for me.
I know they did not go silently,
I know that we have come to dis
Because too many people are staying silent.

The silences are painful,
They make me nervous,
I fear falling over
Or being captured and made a slave
So I will not close my eyes.
I look at the floor for ten seconds
I look to my left for ten seconds
I look to my right for ten seconds,

I spend ten seconds scanning the room
Looking for someone that looks like my mother,
I spend ten seconds looking for spies
And ten seconds are spent looking at the person
Who called the one minute of silence,
And I wonder how do they count their minute?
I always spend the extra seconds
Looking for people I know,
Wondering how long they will live.

I spend hours considering our trials and
Tribulations
I seem to have spent a lifetime
Thinking about death;
Rolan Adams
Will not leave me.
I've tried to look at dis scientifically
I've tried to look at dis religiously,
But I don't want to limit myself either way,
I've spent so much time standing in silence,
It reminds me of being in trouble
In the headmaster's office,
Waiting for the judgement.
I've spent hours
Standing for minutes
Pondering the meaning of life

The reason for death
And considering my time and space.

Benjamin Zephaniah (1958–)

Chosen by Mike Mansfield and Yvette Vanson

This comes from a collection of poems by Benjamin Zephaniah published in 2001, entitled *Too Black Too Strong*. We chose it because contemporary poetry rarely displays political force, insight and humour. We have been lucky enough to know Benjamin as a friend and to experience his commitment first hand. Having spent a year as 'poet in residence' at my chambers – Tooks Court – this particular poem embraces all the names of those who have fuelled the struggle against prejudice, bigotry, oppression and racism.

GIORNO DEI MORTI

Along the avenue of cypresses,
All in their scarlet cloaks and surplices
Of linen, go the chanting choristers,
The priests in gold and black, the villagers . . .

And all along the path to the cemetery
The round dark heads of men crowd silently,
And black-scarved faces of womenfolk, wistfully
Watch at the banner of death, and the mystery.

And at the foot of a grave a father stands
With sunken head, and forgotten, folded hands;
And at the foot of a grave a mother kneels
With pale shut face, nor either hears nor feels

The coming of the chanting choristers
Between the avenue of cypresses,
The silence of the many villagers,
The candle-flames beside the surplices.

D. H. Lawrence (1885–1930)

Chosen by Robert Lindsay

I always choose this poem as one of my favourites and people say 'How depressing!' For me it is a poem I have grown to understand. I had to learn it by rote at the age of fifteen – never fully understanding the complexities of the language. Because it is so firmly fixed in my head I have found that its imagery has got clearer and clearer as I have got older and know what it is to experience the death of a loved one.

AND DEATH SHALL HAVE NO DOMINION

And death shall have no dominion.
Dead men naked they shall be one
With the man in the wind and the west moon;
When their bones are picked clean and the clean bones gone,
They shall have stars at elbow and foot;
Though they go mad they shall be sane,
Though they sink through the sea they shall rise again;
Though lovers be lost love shall not;
And death shall have no dominion.

And death shall have no dominion.
Under the windings of the sea
They lying long shall not die windily;
Twisting on racks when sinews give way,
Strapped to a wheel, yet they shall not break;
Faith in their hands shall snap in two,
And the unicorn evils run them through;
Split all ends up they shan't crack;
And death shall have no dominion.

And death shall have no dominion.
No more may gulls cry at their ears
Or waves break loud on the seashores;
Where blew a flower may a flower no more
Lift its head to the blows of the rain;
Though they be mad and dead as nails,
Heads of the characters hammer through daisies;
Break in the sun till the sun breaks down,
And death shall have no dominion.

Dylan Thomas (1914–1953)

I like the poem for its defiant attitude to death. The images of the physical power, the destruction that inevitably does for us all, contrasted with the beauty of renewal and rebirth. 'Though lovers be lost love shall not' is such a fine, stirring and memorable line.

FIDELE

Fear no more the heat o' the sun,
   Nor the furious winter's rages;
Thou thy worldly task hast done,
   Home art gone, and ta'en thy wages:
Golden lads and girls all must,
As chimney-sweepers, come to dust.

Fear no more the frown o' the great,
   Thou art past the tyrant's stroke;
Care no more to clothe and eat;
   To thee the reed is as the oak:
The sceptre, learning, physic, must
All follow this, and come to dust.

Fear no more the lightning-flash,
   Nor the all-dreaded thunder-stone;
Fear not slander, censure rash;
   Thou hast finish'd joy and moan:
All lovers young, all lovers must
Consign to thee, and come to dust.

No exorciser harm thee!
   Nor no witchcraft charm thee!
Ghost unlaid forbear thee!
   Nothing ill come near thee!
Quiet consummation have;
And renownèd be thy grave!

William Shakespeare (1564–1616)

Chosen by Tony Robinson

Defiance in the face of death, laughter in the teeth of suffering.

The implicated generations made
This symbol of their lives, a stone made light
By what is carved on it.
                              The plaiting masks,
But not with involutions of a shade,
What a stone says and what a stone cross asks.

Something that is not mirrored by nor trapped
In webs of water or bag-nets of cloud;
The tangled mesh of weed
                              lets it go by.
Only men's minds could ever have unmapped
Into abstraction such a territory.

No green bay going yellow over sand
Is written on by winds to tell a tale
Of death-dishevelled gull
                              or heron, stiff
As a cruel clerk with gaunt writs in his hand
– Or even of light, that makes its depths a cliff.

Singing responses order otherwise.
The tangled generations ravelled out
In links of song whose sweet
                              strong choruses
Are these stone involutions to the eyes
Given to the ear in abstract vocables.

The stone remains, and the cross, to let us know
Their unjust, hard demands, as symbols do.
But on them twine and grow

                          beneath the dove
        Serpents of wisdom whose cool statements show
        Such understanding that it seems like love.

                                   Norman MacCaig (1910–96)

Chosen by James Naughtie

It takes a poet to turn a piece of stone into a vibrant reflection of humanity,
carrying the story of generations. Norman MacCaig is one of my favourite
poets because he describes the instinctive embrace between the human world
and its surroundings. When I read him now – as when I used to listen to
him in Scotland reading aloud – I'm transported to a place that's usually
out of reach. He's a poet who is always trying to describe what it is to
be human.

ELEGY WRITTEN IN
A COUNTRY CHURCHYARD

The curfew tolls the knell of parting day,
  The lowing herd wind slowly o'er the lea,
The plowman homeward plods his weary way,
  And leaves the world to darkness and to me.

Now fades the glimmering landscape on the sight,
  And all the air a solemn stillness holds,
Save where the beetle wheels his droning flight,
  And drowsy tinklings lull the distant folds.

Save that from yonder ivy-mantled tower
  The moping owl does to the moon complain
Of such as, wandering near her secret bower,
  Molest her ancient solitary reign.

Beneath those rugged elms, that yew-tree's shade,
  Where heaves the turf in many a mouldering heap,
Each in his narrow cell for ever laid,
  The rude forefathers of the hamlet sleep.

The breezy call of incense-breathing morn,
  The swallow twittering from the straw-built shed,
The cock's shrill clarion, or the echoing horn,
  No more shall rouse them from their lowly bed.

For them no more the blazing hearth shall burn,
  Or busy housewife ply her evening care:
No children run to lisp their sire's return,
  Or climb his knee the envied kiss to share.

Oft did the harvest to their sickle yield,
  Their furrow of the stubborn glebe has broke:

How jocund did they drive their team afield!
    How bowed the woods beneath their sturdy stroke!

Let not ambition mock their useful toil,
    Their homely joys, and destiny obscure;
Nor grandeur hear with a disdainful smile
    The short and simple annals of the poor.

The boast of heraldry, the pomp of power,
    And all that beauty, all that wealth e'er gave,
Awaits alike the inevitable hour.
    The paths of glory lead but to the grave.

Nor you, ye proud, impute to these the fault,
    If memory o'er their tomb no trophies raise,
Where through the long-drawn aisle and fretted vault
    The pealing anthem swells the note of praise.

Can storied urn or animated bust
    Back to its mansion call the fleeting breath?
Can honour's voice provoke the silent dust,
    Or flattery soothe the dull cold ear of death?

Perhaps in this neglected spot is laid
    Some heart once pregnant with celestial fire;
Hands, that the rod of empire might have swayed
    Or waked to extasy the living lyre.

But knowledge to their eyes her ample page
    Rich with the spoils of time did ne'er unroll;
Chill penury repressed their noble rage,
    And froze the genial current of the soul.

Full many a gem of purest ray serene,
    The dark unfathomed caves of ocean bear;

Full many a flower is born to blush unseen,
   And waste its sweetness on the desert air.

Some village-Hampden, that with dauntless breast
   The little tyrant of his fields withstood,
Some mute inglorious Milton here may rest,
   Some Cromwell guiltless of his country's blood

The applause of listening senates to command.
   The threats of pain and ruin to despise,
To scatter plenty o'er a smiling land,
   And read their history in a nation's eyes,

Their lot forbad: nor circumscribed alone
   Their growing virtues, but their crimes confined;
Forbad to wade through slaughter to a throne,
   And shut the gates of mercy on mankind,

The struggling pangs of conscious truth to hide,
   To quench the blushes of ingenuous shame,
Or heap the shrine of luxury and pride
   With incense kindled at the Muse's flame.

Far from the madding crowd's ignoble strife,
   Their sober wishes never learned to stray;
Along the cool sequestered vale of life
   They kept the noiseless tenor of their way.

Yet even those bones from insult to protect
   Some frail memorial still erected nigh,
With uncouth rhymes and shapeless sculpture decked,
   Implores the passing tribute of a sigh.

Their name, their years, spelt by the unlettered Muse,
   The place of fame and elegy supply:

And many a holy text around she strews,
     That teach the rustic moralist to die.

For who, to dumb forgetfulness a prey,
     This pleasing anxious being e'er resigned,
Left the warm precincts of the cheerful day,
     Nor cast one longing lingering look behind?

On some fond breast the parting soul relies,
     Some pious drops the closing eye requires;
E'en from the tomb the voice of nature cries,
     E'en in our ashes live their wonted fires.

For thee, who mindful of the unhonoured dead,
     Dost in these lines their artless tale relate;
If chance, by lonely contemplation led,
     Some kindred spirit shall inquire thy fate –

Haply some hoary-headed swain may say,
     'Oft have we seen him at the peep of dawn
Brushing with hasty steps the dews away
     To meet the sun upon the upland lawn.

'There at the foot of yonder nodding beech,
     That wreathes its old fantastic roots so high,
His listless length at noontide would he stretch,
     And pore upon the brook that babbles by.

'Hard by yon wood, now smiling as in scorn,
     Muttering his wayward fancies he would rove,
Now drooping, woeful-wan, like one forlorn,
     Or crazed with care, or crossed in hopeless love.

'One morn I missed him on the customed hill,
     Along the heath, and near his favourite tree;
Another came; nor yet beside the rill,
     Nor up the lawn, nor at the wood was he:

'The next, with dirges due in sad array
    Slow through the church-way path we saw him borne.
Approach and read (for thou can'st read) the lay,
    Graved on the stone beneath yon aged thorn.'

(There scattered oft, the earliest of the year,
    By hands unseen, are showers of violets found:
The redbreast loves to bill and warble there,
    And little footsteps lightly print the ground.)

The Epitaph

Here rests his head upon the lap of Earth
    A Youth, to Fortune and to Fame unknown.
Fair Science frowned not on his humble birth,
    And Melancholy marked him for her own.

Large was his bounty, and his soul sincere,
    Heaven did a recompense as largely send;
He gave to Misery all he had, a tear,
    He gained from Heaven ('twas all he wished) a friend.

No farther seek his merits to disclose,
    Or draw his frailties from their dread abode,
(There they alike in trembling hope repose.)
    The bosom of his Father and his God.

Thomas Gray (1716–71)

Chosen by Tim Smit

Gray's timeless lines celebrate the virtues and the often unrealised potential of men and women whose coming and passing remain largely unremarked, except in St Ewe and thousands of communities like it. On the other hand, as de Gaulle's wry comment had it, the graveyards of the world are full of irreplaceable men.

GRANDEUR OF GHOSTS

When I have heard small talk about great men
I climb to bed; light my two candles; then
Consider what was said; and put aside
What Such-a-one remarked and Someone-else replied.

They have spoken lightly of my deathless friends,
(Lamps for my gloom, hands guiding where I stumble,)
Quoting, for shallow conversational ends,
What Shelley shrilled, what Blake once wildly muttered . . .

How can they use such names and be not humble?
I have sat silent; angry at what they uttered.
The dead bequeathed them life; the dead have said
What these can only memorize and mumble.

Siegfried Sassoon (1886–1967)

Chosen by Tom Conti

I always want to break into this at dinner parties.

DIVING INTO THE WRECK

First having read the book of myths,
and loaded the camera,
and checked the edge of the knife-blade,
I put on
the body-armor of black rubber
the absurd flippers
the grave and awkward mask.
I am having to do this
not like Cousteau with his
assiduous team
aboard the sun-flooded schooner
but here alone.

There is a ladder.
The ladder is always there
hanging innocently
close to the side of the schooner.
We know what it is for,
we who have used it.
Otherwise
it's a piece of maritime floss
some sundry equipment.

I go down.
Rung after rung and still
the oxygen immerses me
the blue light
the clear atoms
of our human air.
I go down.
My flippers cripple me,
I crawl like an insect down the ladder
and there is no one

to tell me when the ocean
will begin.

First the air is blue and then
it is bluer and then green and then
black I am blacking out and yet
my mask is powerful
it pumps my blood with power
the sea is another story
the sea is not a question of power
I have to learn alone
to turn my body without force
in the deep element.

And now: it is easy to forget
what I came for
among so many who have always
lived here
swaying their crenellated fans
between the reefs
and besides
you breathe differently down here.

I came to explore the wreck.
The words are purposes.
The words are maps.
I came to see the damage that was done
and the treasures that prevail.
I stroke the beam of my lamp
slowly along the flank
of something more permanent
than fish or weed

the thing I came for:
the wreck and not the story of the wreck
the thing itself and not the myth
the drowned face always staring
toward the sun
the evidence of damage
worn by salt and sway into this threadbare beauty
the ribs of the disaster
curving their assertion
among the tentative haunters.

This is the place.
And I am here, the mermaid whose dark hair
streams black, the merman in his armored body
We circle silently
about the wreck
we dive into the hold.
I am she: I am he

whose drowned face sleeps with open eyes
whose breasts still bear the stress
whose silver, copper, vermeil cargo lies
obscurely inside barrels
half-wedged and left to rot
we are the half-destroyed instruments
that once held to a course
the water-eaten log
the fouled compass

We are, I am, you are
by cowardice or courage
the one who find our way
back to this scene

carrying a knife, a camera
a book of myths
in which
our names do not appear.

Adrienne Rich (1929–)

Chosen by Margaret Atwood

REMEMBER

Remember me when I am gone away,
    Gone far away into the silent land;
    When you can no more hold me by the hand,
Nor I half turn to go yet turning stay.
Remember me when no more day by day
    You tell me of our future that you planned:
    Only remember me; you understand
It will be late to counsel then or pray.
Yet if you should forget me for a while
    And afterwards remember, do not grieve:
    For if the darkness and corruption leave
    A vestige of the thoughts that once I had,
Better by far you should forget and smile
    Than that you should remember and be sad.

Christina Rossetti (1830–94)

Chosen by Greta Scacchi

on exile and the refugee

To a refugee,
What is this, a poem?
Drop it from a hundred feet,
The children sent
To scavenge the plain
Would mistake it
For the wrapper on
A peanut butter ration
But pick it up the same.
The father at the camp
Would hold it
Up to the light,
And seeing the foreign language,
Dust it off and
Tuck it by his side:
Perhaps this paper
Could secure free passage
To his boyhood land.
The old man, his father,
Lying in the tent
Would once have spoken English
But be blind.

You reader,
Yes, you reader
With this poem in your hand,
It is addressed to you,
That when you have read it
You will look to the sky
With the sensation we get now
On hearing a low plane go over.

Andrew Darnton, 2001

Chosen by the Editor

CONCERNING THE LABEL EMIGRANT

I always found the name false which they gave us: Emigrants.
That means those who leave their country. But we
Did not leave, of our own free will
Choosing another land. Nor did we enter
Into a land, to stay there, if possible for ever.
Merely, we fled. We are driven out, banned.
Not a home, but an exile, shall the land be that took us in.
Restlessly we wait thus, as near as we can to the frontier
Awaiting the day of return, every smallest alteration
Observing beyond the boundary, zealously asking
Every arrival, forgetting nothing and giving up nothing
And also not forgiving anything which happened, forgiving
       nothing.
Ah, the silence of the Sound does not deceive us! We hear
       the shrieks
From their camps even here. Yes, we ourselves
Are almost like rumours of crimes, which escaped
Over the frontier. Every one of us
Who with torn shoes walks through the crowd
Bears witness to the shame which now defiles our land.
But none of us
Will stay here. The final word
Is yet unspoken.

Bertolt Brecht (1898–1956); translated by Stephen Spender

Chosen by Tom Wilkinson

WRETCHEDNESS

My soul is bored of the repetition
      of days and nights,
My heart tired, my problems unsolved;
But still that bitter, black hope,
Like a broken dagger,
       remains in my breast.

In the demon-land of my existence
There is a life-giving,
      pain-fostering secret
      burning;
I keep myself alive by concealing
      that secret
With a thousand flaming wounds.

My lips are sealed like some old scar
Lest this secret should devour me again;
I show a sullen face lest the inquisitive
Should fall on me
      with their powerful resentment.

The sunshine finds no way
      through my solitude,
It is all darkness, cold and lostness;
I am sick of the dusk at sunset
And of light at the break of dawn.

I am living death in my sorrows,
Though in company of the living
      I share their noisy joys;

Beware of my wretchedness, beware!
I am a man who makes love
        with the corpse of his dead hope.

Fereydun Tavallali (1919–85)

Chosen by Brian Eno

Imagine that you see the wretched strangers,
Their babies at their backs, with their poor luggage
Plodding to th' ports and coasts for transportation,
And that you sit as kings in your desires,
Authority quite silenced by your brawl
And you in ruff of your opinions clothed:
What had you got? I'll tell you. You had taught
How insolence and strong hand should prevail,
How order should be quelled – and by this pattern
Not one of you should live an aged man,
For other ruffians as their fancies wrought
With selfsame hand, self reasons, and self right
Would shark on you, and men like ravenous fishes
Would feed on one another.

Lines attributed to William Shakespeare (1564–1616)

Chosen by David Calder

Shakespeare's warning that what is visited by the strong upon the weak may at some other time be paid for in kind sounds through all history: 'If they come for me in the morning they will come for you at night.' We tolerate xenophobia, racism and poverty at our peril. The disaster of September 11th and the ensuing war did not come unexpected 'out of a clear blue sky' – it came murderously from our indifference and inhumanity to each other.

WIND

This is the wind, the wind in a field of corn.
Great crowds are fleeing from a major disaster
Down the long valleys, the green swaying wadis,
Down through the beautiful catastrophe of wind.

Families, tribes, nations and their livestock
Have heard something, seen something. An expectation
Or a gigantic misunderstanding has swept over the hilltop
Bending the ear of the hedgerow with stories of fire and sword.

I saw a thousand years pass in two seconds.
Land was lost, languages rose and divided.
This lord went east and found safety.
His brother sought Africa and a dish of aloes.

Centuries, minutes later, one might ask
How the hilt of a sword wandered so far from the smithy.
And somewhere they will sing: 'Like chaff we were borne
In the wind.' This is the wind in a field of corn.

James Fenton (1949–)

Chosen by Wendy Cope

PATRIOTIC POEM AGAINST NATIONALISM

for a newborn child

1

Is it too bright for you, darling?
Under the yews in the churchyard
Inland from the town, into the hills, up the lanes
It is cool and green-shadowed and quiet;   and there

LYETH the Bodi of Ann David
Who died the 21st January 1784
Aged one month – so born just about Christmas.
And you are two days, born into flaming June.

2

Many the infant children buried here
Beneath elaborate tiles, and graved slate
Polished hard and clean with the lettering
As clear as the day it was done.

Memorials, important, memories solid
For each little scrap of throw-away life
Slate thick and heavy as marble, but dimmer
And, absorbing the light, seeming more part of the earth.
The hillside sleeps in the morning sun, in the years
Of sleep that has come to this place.

Beyond the shaded porch-path, out in the field
Light pours unwinking on the bright new graves.

3

'Genth' I shall call you, who have no Welsh in you.
Little Welsh girl, little scrap born in Wales.
We have no Welsh in us, and I no drop of Celtic.
But I more than you likely to learn these stones
And I, for no reason, more likely to learn this language.

4

To the traveller
Any place they come to can be home
Even for a day or two
And any language learnt can be our own
For as long as we care to use it, can be
In that we all are strangers somewhere.
Everything we know
We have to learn, even what we are,
Become the part we practise.

You come from wandering people much attached
To places here and there, and fed by roots
(What that lives isn't?) but like water lilies
Floating in moving streams
That take and give back wherever they find themselves;
          from people attached to the day
Wherever it fades or opens. The same light
Flowing round somewhere else will make you blink,
As you do now, gossamer, so frail, so silken,
Force you to come to terms, force you to stir.

5

Later you will get
Particulars: names nationalities opinions,
A history, and be pulled along the track
Your people make to travel on.
                                              Now
It is just life and air and the June sun
Shining by the sea on Wales,
A morsel of flesh and its light breathing,
Gossamer-light for life, durable,
Tough as thistle-down or the fair hair of the dandelions
Seeding to make the inextirpable roots
That fill the banks with flowers.

6

I drive from dark shadows up into light again
The sun hitting my mirror
Plunged into dazzle of darkness I continue half blind
Until sight settles.
We swing from dark to light to dark, swaying
Between the Poles
We clutch, we scream   and you, tiny slip,
Take it all so quietly. You are so calm
Blinking, adjusting, your blood settling no doubt
To pulse at its own speed now, in its separate world.
It has been dark where you have come from
Dark and quiet like the churchyard on the hill
Drowsing in noontide, dark surrounded by light.

Too much is put on children by our wishes:
To carry the banner, to forge and protect the nation,
To make Utopia, which we could not do.
We really should not wish you anything
Except good luck and health and the wit to use them.
But – old ritualist – I want my wishes.
I wish you may
Avoid being mired by the past or the claim of sects;
Not lose the sense of history, but loose
The clutch of the bitter ghosts unsettled people
Feed with acrid blood, as some keep dogs
Hungry on the highway.
It is for such as you who everywhere
Turn to their mother's milk, try out the air,
Move away from the glare, that if we could
We would change nations into geography.

I hope you will love whatever place you live in
Because you love it, not because commanded
By joyless people gritting their teeth for power;
Welcomed everywhere, and safe enough
To welcome others and like them for their strangeness.
This is for later,

                    for now
Welcome, strange darling, into this new place
Where you have lighted, soft and quiet as thistledown
To thrive wherever you land, Madog, my girl from Wales.

Jenny Joseph (1932–)

THOUGHTS ON THE DURATION OF EXILE

I

Don't drive a nail in the wall –
you can chuck your coat over a chair.
Why so much care for four days?
Tomorrow you'll be back home.

Leave the little sapling without water –
why plant yet another tree?
Before it's as high as that little step there
you'll be laughing far away.

Pull your cap over your face when folk go by!
Why thumb through a foreign grammar?
The message to call you home again
will be couched in a language you know.

The way plaster falls from the ceiling
(Do nothing about that either!)
those iron railings will crumble away
set up at the frontier
by force against justice.

II

Now look at the nail you've driven in the wall:
when do you think you'll be back home?
Would you like to know what you really think?

Day after day
you work for liberation

sitting in your room and writing away.
Would you like to know what you think about your work?
How about the way you've kept watering
the little chestnut-tree in the corner of the yard!

Bertolt Brecht (1898–1956); translated by Harry Guest

Chosen by Christopher Hampton

A strange grey town
Blotted out by night;
Deep voids of crowded air,
A flickering neon sign,
A deserted platform.
Across the other side,
On red benches no-one sits.
The box clock ticks, echoes
In the brimming space.
Flick, a minute passes.

But more –
People hurry to rain flecked cars
Enclosed in metal,
Relieved and going home.
An image of evening –
Television, warmth, food.
People beyond yellow squares,
Who see no rivulet stranger.
A barrier of space makes her
Untouchable.
(Sitting in the dust, fierce sun,
Fire wounds sweet smelling death)

And more –
People drain away to duvets
The streets, full of no-one,
Transform.
As her tired footsteps pass,
Blank building faces
Are dispassionate judges.
Under their gaze, people
Draw in, shiver, scurry

To bolt holes, protection.
Hurry in the hostile air.
Night streets are no place for people.

And more.
Yellow black clouds
Blanket thick, sinking
Sludge on the station.
And trains, vast heaves
Of agonising noise –
A flicker of faces, coffee cups,
Framed by black –
Flick flick flick swoosh
Gone. Wind in her fingers.
The dark resignation hunches.
There are no trains stop here tonight.

Sophie Large (1978–98)

Chosen by Peter Bowles

I chose this poem because I wanted this young woman's memory to live on as her tragedy somehow is the tragedy of so many young people. Fortunately she writes of her joys of youth and life in her published diary and poems, *Sophie's Log*. She was nineteen when she died.

The loneliness and alienation of the lone traveller surrounded by people going about their business had some feeling of the refugee.

TO A MOUSE,

On turning her up in her Nest, with the Plough, November 1785

Wee, sleeket, cowran, tim'rous *beastie*,
O, what a panic's in thy breastie!
Thou need na start awa sae hasty,
　　　Wi' bickering brattle!
I wad be laith to rin an' chase thee,
　　　Wi' murd'ring *pattle!*

I'm truly sorry Man's dominion
Has broken Nature's social union,
An' justifies that ill opinion,
　　　Which makes thee startle,
At me, thy poor, earth-born companion,
　　　An' *fellow-mortal!*

I doubt na, whyles, but thou may *thieve;*
What then? poor beastie, thou maun live!
A *daimen-icker* in a *thrave*
　　　'S a sma' request:
I'll get a blessin wi' the lave,
　　　An' never miss't!

Thy wee-bit *housie*, too, in ruin!
It's silly wa's the win's are strewin!
An' naething, now, to big a new ane,
　　　O' foggage green!
An' bleak *December's winds* ensuin,
　　　Baith snell an' keen!

Thou saw the fields laid bare an' wast,
An' weary *Winter* comin fast,
An' cozie here, beneath the blast,

Thou thought to dwell,
Till crash! the cruel *coulter* past
Out thro' thy cell.

That wee-bit heap o' leaves an stibble,
Has cost thee monie a weary nibble!
Now thou's turn'd out, for a' thy trouble,
But house or hald,
To thole the Winter's *sleety dribble*,
An' *cranreuch* cauld!

But Mousie, thou art no thy-lane,
In proving *foresight* may be vain:
The best laid schemes o' *Mice* an' *Men*
Gang aft agley,
An' lea'e us nought but grief an' pain,
For promis'd joy!

Still, thou art blest, compar'd wi' *me*!
The *present* only toucheth thee:
But Och! I *backward* cast my e'e,
On prospects drear!
An' *forward*, tho' I canna *see*,
I *guess* an' *fear*!

Robert Burns (1759–96)

Chosen by Seamus Heaney

Robert Burns's 'To a Mouse' is about the unreliability of the world, a poem in which a flash-flood of pity and terror comes and goes through the poet's consciousness and leaves him changed. When I first read it as a schoolboy, I was susceptible to the tenderness of the speech and the lovely fellow-feeling it expresses, but as I grow older and realise what the 'cruel coulter' of history can do, I value it more and more for its tragic force. The 'bleak December's winds' blow as fatally across the Ayrshire field as the storm blows across the heath in *King Lear*, and to similar effect. The old king and the young ploughman are exposed to what W. B. Yeats called 'the desolation of reality'. Still, the great thing about the poem is the way it can warm the heart and face the music at one and the same time.

BOY WITH ORANGE: OUT OF KOSOVO

A boy holding an orange in his hands
Has crossed the border in uncertainty.

He stands there, stares with marble eyes at scenes
Too desolate for him to comprehend.

Now, in this globe he's clutching something safe,
A round assurance and a promised joy

No-one shall take away. He cannot smile.
Behind him are the stones of babyhood.

Soon he will find a hand, perhaps, to hold,
Or a kind face, some comfort for a while.

Lotte Kramer (1923–)

Chosen by Harry Eyres

The succulent, glowing orange the boy clutches in this poem contrasts with
the hard greyness of the stones he leaves behind (the rubble of destruction)
and his marble eyes. It would be too simple to call it 'a symbol of hope'; it
is a reality, a principle of life and health as real as the murderous violence
he has grown up amidst. Uncertainty is the key word: who knows what
life will bring this boy, but perhaps he has not lost the human power to
imagine the better when faced with the worst.

Lotte Kramer was herself a child refugee when she arrived in Britain from
Germany in 1939.

THE OWL

Downhill I came, hungry, and yet not starved;
Cold, yet had heat within me that was proof
Against the North wind; tired, yet so that rest
Had seemed the sweetest thing under a roof.

Then at the inn I had food, fire, and rest,
Knowing how hungry, cold, and tired was I.
All of the night was quite barred out except
An owl's cry, a most melancholy cry

Shaken out long and clear upon the hill,
No merry note, nor cause of merriment,
But one telling me plain what I escaped
And others could not, that night, as in I went.

And salted was my food, and my repose,
Salted and sobered, too, by the bird's voice
Speaking for all who lay under the stars,
Soldiers and poor, unable to rejoice.

Edward Thomas (1878–1917)

Chosen by Edwin Morgan

'The Owl' is a fine evocation of the lives of all those who are hungry or homeless or caught in a war situation.

I'm writing out this poem
To show just how I feel
To all the poorest people
Who can't eat a proper meal.

I feel so very sorry
When I think about you,
I know if it were me
I would hate it too.

For home's a loving shelter
Away from all you fear
Because you know that all your
Friends and family are near

So try to keep your hopes up
When you are feeling down
Because you know that friends like me
Will love you all year round.

Cecily Haywood, aged eight

THE EMBRACE

Warm me this night,
O my trust in freedom
wrap me warm
against my mattress thin and blanket torn.
Out there is unimaginable cold and wind,
outside – oppression,
torture,
out there – death.
O my trust in freedom
enter deep,
warm me through this night.
On my palm a place is ready
for your hands,
on my thighs a place
to lean your knees.
Enclose me,
sheathe me,
wrap me warm,
O my trust in freedom
wrap me warm this night.

Oktay Rifat (1914–88); translated by Ruth Christie

Chosen by Juliet Stevenson

There are many more well-known poems I could have suggested, but the poetry of Oktay Rifat came as a discovery to me recently, so I thought others might like to discover him too. A towering figure in modern Turkish poetry, his work is full of faith in optimism, in the essential goodness of humankind, in the mind's power to hear and to heal.

ALL YOU WHO SLEEP TONIGHT

All you who sleep tonight
Far from the ones you love
No hand to left or right,
And emptiness above –

Know that you aren't alone.
The whole world shares your fears,
Some for two nights or one,
And some for all their years.

Vikram Seth (1952–)

Chosen by Felicity Kendal

on diversity

HUMAN FAMILY

I note the obvious differences
in the human family.
Some of us are serious,
some thrive on comedy.

Some declare their lives are lived
as true profundity,
and others claim they really live
the real reality.

The variety of our skin tones
can confuse, bemuse, delight,
brown and pink and beige and purple,
tan and blue and white.

I've sailed upon the seven seas
and stopped in every land,
I've seen the wonders of the world,
Not yet one common man.

I know ten thousand women
called Jane and Mary Jane,
but I've not seen any two
who really were the same.

Mirror twins are different
although their features jibe,
and lovers think quite different thoughts
while lying side by side.

We love and lose in China,
we weep on England's moors,

and laugh and moan in Guinea,
and thrive on Spanish shores.

We seek success in Finland,
are born and die in Maine.
In minor ways we differ,
in major we're the same.

I note the obvious differences
between each sort and type,
but we are more alike, my friends,
than we are unalike.

We are more alike, my friends,
than we are unalike.

We are more alike, my friends,
than we are unalike.

Maya Angelou (1928–)

Chosen by Pauline Quirke

I think this just about says it all.

FIRST THEY CAME FOR THE JEWS

First they came for the Jews
and I did not speak out –
because I was not a Jew
Then they came for the communists
and I did not speak out –
because I was not a communist
Then they came for the Trade Unionists
and I did not speak out –
because I was not a Trade Unionist
Then they came for me –
and there was no one left
to speak out for me.

Pastor Martin Niemöller (1892–1984); translated by H. Schiff

Chosen by Sue Townsend

There is no choice. It has to be this one.

WHEN I WAS IN CHINA

I saw the whole world of commerce
and democracy and free-marketry gone mad
in one Ugly American, lining his Levis with
silk to stop the chafing
so he could walk along the Great Wall.

Further south, in one magnificent moment,
when a whole village appeared
as soft and gentle as a Chinese water-colour,
he looked around and said 'It doesn't seem like they're
having much recreational sex around here.'

Fay Hart

Chosen by Hugo Williams

this is thi
six a clock
news thi
man said n
thi reason
a talk wia
BBC accent
iz coz yi
widny wahnt
mi ti talk
aboot thi
trooth wia
voice lik
waana yoo
scruff. If
a toktaboot
thi trooth
lik waana yoo
scruff yi
widny thingk
it wuz troo.
jist wanna yoo
scruff tokn.
thirz a right
way ti spell
ana right way
ti tok it. this
is me tokn yir
right way a
spellin. this
is ma trooth.
yooz doant no
thi trooth

yirsellz cawz
yi canny talk
right. this is
the six a clock
nyooz. belt up.

Tom Leonard (1944–)

Chosen by John Hegley

This piece suggests ideas relevant to refugee status: fitting in, feeling wanted,
retaining dignity and identity and being able to make a joke about it all.

THE ENGLISH ARE SO NICE!

The English are so nice
so awfully nice
they're the nicest people in the world.
And what's more, they're very nice about being nice
about your being nice as well!
If you're not nice they soon make you feel it.

Americans and French and Germans and so on
they're all very well
but they're not *really* nice, you know.
They're not nice in *our* sense of the word, are they now?

That's why one doesn't have to take them seriously.
We must be nice to them, of course,
of course, naturally –
But it doesn't really matter what you say to them,
they don't really understand –
you can just say anything to them:
be nice, you know, just be nice
but you must never take them seriously, they wouldn't understand,
just be nice, you know! oh, fairly nice,
not too nice of course, they take advantage –
but nice enough, just nice enough
to let them feel they're not quite as nice as they might be.

D. H. Lawrence (1885–1930)

Chosen by Ben Kingsley

Lawrence was a great Englishman with a scale of imagination, vision and expression. He hated complacency, xenophobia and that false sense of cultural superiority we the English can display. A very witty, thought-provoking poem.

A coincidence must be
Part of a whole chain
Whose links are unknown to me.

I feel them round me
Everywhere I go: in queues,
In trains, under bridges,

People, or coincidences, flukes
of logic which fail
Because of me, because

We move singly through streets,
The last of some sad species,
Pacing the floors of zoos,

Our luck homing forever
Backwards through grasses
To the brink of another time.

Hugo Williams (1941–)

PHOTO IN ST JAMES' PARK

a hot spring day by the lake
and a young woman and man
probably tourists
possibly Spanish
who wanted a photo of themselves together
handed their camera to someone
almost definitely English
who certain fellow countrymen
might predictably describe
as a very drunken old dosser
but to them he was just a passer by
he accepted the camera
took a long time focusing
and steadying himself
but managed to take the picture
and received genuine gratitude
from the two
who had seen nothing
deviant in his behaviour
and who would remember him
as a friendly and helpful
English gentleman
if he hadn't fallen in the lake
with their camera.

John Hegley (1953–)

Chosen by Richard Wilson

I've long admired the work of John Hegley for his mastery of the language, his compassion and, of course, his great wit.

THIS ABOVE ALL IS PRECIOUS
AND REMARKABLE

This above all is precious and remarkable,
How we put ourselves in one another's care,
How in spite of everything we trust each other.

Fishermen at whatever point they are dipping and lifting
On the dark green swell they partly think of as home
Hear the gale warnings that fly to them like gulls.

The scientists study the weather for love of studying it,
And not specially for love of the fishermen,
And the wireless engineers do the transmission for love of wireless,

But how it adds up is that when the terrible white malice
Of the waves high as cliffs is let loose to seek a victim,
The fishermen are somewhere else and so not drowned.

And why should this chain of miracles be easier to believe
Than that my darling should come home to me as naturally
As she trusts a restaurant not to poison her?

They are simple examples of well-known types of miracle,
The two of them,
That can happen at any time of the day or night.

John Wain (1925–94)

Chosen by Judi Dench

The poem was sent to me and it struck some sort of chord in me. I am
sending it to you in the hope that it will strike a chord in someone else.

on innocence and experience

NURSERY RHYME OF
INNOCENCE AND EXPERIENCE

I had a silver penny
    And an apricot tree
And I said to the sailor
    On the white quay

'Sailor O sailor
    Will you bring me
If I give you my penny
    And my apricot tree

A fez from Algeria
    An Arab drum to beat
A little gilt sword
    And a parakeet?'

And he smiled and he kissed me
    As strong as death
And I saw his red tongue
    And I felt his sweet breath

'You may keep your penny
    And your apricot tree
And I'll bring your presents
    Back from sea.'

O the ship dipped down
    On the rim of the sky
And I waited while three
    Long summers went by

Then one steel morning
    On the white quay

I saw a grey ship
  Come in from sea

Slowly she came
  Across the bay
For her flashing rigging
  Was shot away

All round her wake
  The seabirds cried
And flew in and out
  Of the hole in her side

Slowly she came
  In the path of the sun
And I heard the sound
  Of a distant gun

And a stranger came running
  Up to me
From the deck of the ship
  And he said, said he

'O are you the boy
  Who would wait on the quay
With the silver penny
  And the apricot tree?

I've a plum-coloured fez
  And a drum for thee
And a sword and a parakeet
  From over the sea.'

'O where is the sailor
  With bold red hair?

And what is that volley
  On the bright air?

O where are the other
  Girls and boys?
And why have you brought me
  Children's toys?'

Charles Causley (1917–)

Chosen by Griff Rhys Jones

The poem pretty much speaks for itself. It is simple and direct. It trips along like the nursery rhyme of the title, but the naïve style releases something rather more complicated. The rhythm is urgent and oddly demanding: a strident beating (try reading it aloud). And touches like 'his red tongue' and 'sweet breath' have a delicious sense of unease. The final couplet never fails to get me. Causley loved the ballad form and this is an early example of his unerring ability to hide bitter truths in it. This is a deceptively grown-up poem about growing up.

THE TOYS

My little Son, who look'd from thoughtful eyes
And moved and spoke in quiet grown-up wise,
Having my law the seventh time disobey'd,
I struck him, and dismissd
With hard words and unkiss'd,
His Mother, who was patient, being dead.
Then, fearing lest his grief should hinder sleep,
I visited his bed,
But found him slumbering deep,
With darken'd eyelids, and their lashes yet
From his late sobbing wet.
And I, with moan,
Kissing away his tears, left others of my own;
For, on a table drawn beside his head,
He had put, within his reach,
A box of counters and a red-vein'd stone,
A piece of glass abraded by the beach
And six or seven shells,
A bottle with bluebells,
And two French copper coins, ranged there with careful art,
To comfort his sad heart.
So when that night I pray'd
To God, I wept, and said:
Ah, when at last we lie with tranced breath,
Not vexing Thee in death,
And Thou rememberest of what toys
We made our joys,
How weakly understood
Thy great commanded good,
Then, fatherly not less

Than I whom Thou hast moulded from the clay,
Thou'lt leave Thy wrath, and say,
'I will be sorry for their childishness.'

Coventry Patmore (1823–96)

Chosen by Timothy West

FERN HILL

Now as I was young and easy under the apple boughs
About the lilting house and happy as the grass was green,
   The night above the dingle starry,
    Time let me hail and climb
   Golden in the heydays of his eyes,
And honoured among wagons I was prince of the apple towns
And once below a time I lordly had the trees and leaves
    Trail with daisies and barley
   Down the rivers of the windfall light.

And as I was green and carefree, famous among the barns
About the happy yard and singing as the farm was home,
   In the sun that is young once only,
    Time let me play and be
   Golden in the mercy of his means,
And green and golden I was huntsman and herdsman, the calves
Sang to my horn, the foxes on the hills barked clear and cold,
    And the sabbath rang slowly
   In the pebbles of the holy streams.

All the sun long it was running, it was lovely, the hay
Fields high as the house, the tunes from the chimneys, it was air
   And playing, lovely and watery
    And fire green as grass.
   And nightly under the simple stars
As I rode to sleep the owls were bearing the farm away,
All the moon long I heard, blessed among stables, the night-jars
   Flying with the ricks, and the horses
    Flashing into the dark.

And then to awake, and the farm, like a wanderer white
With the dew, come back, the cock on his shoulder: it was all
   Shining, it was Adam and maiden,

The sky gathered again
And the sun grew round that very day,
So it must have been after the birth of the simple light
In the first, spinning place, the spellbound horses walking warm
    Out of the whinnying green stable
        On to the fields of praise.

And honoured among foxes and pheasants by the gay house
Under the new made clouds and happy as the heart was long,
    In the sun born over and over,
        I ran my heedless ways,
    My wishes raced through the house high hay
And nothing I cared, at my sky blue trades, that time allows
In all his tuneful turning so few and such morning songs
    Before the children green and golden
        Follow him out of grace.

Nothing I cared, in the lamb white days, that time would take me
Up to the swallow thronged loft by the shadow of my hand,
    In the moon that is always rising,
        Nor that riding to sleep
    I should hear him fly with the high fields
And wake to the farm forever fled from the childless land.
Oh as I was young and easy in the mercy of his means,
    Time held me green and dying
    Though I sang in my chains like the sea.

Dylan Thomas (1914–53)

Chosen by John Humphrys

'Fern Hill' is a great poem and always gives me the sense of hope triumphing
over adversity.

TRANSFORMATION

Suddenly the cherries were there
although I had forgotten
that cherries exist
and caused to be proclaimed: There never have been cherries —
they were there, suddenly and dear.

Plums fell and hit me;
but whoever thinks
that I was transformed
because something fell and hit me
has never been hit by falling plums.

Only when they poured nuts into my shoes
and I had to walk
because the children wanted the kernels
I cried out for cherries, wanted plums
to hit me — and was transformed a little.

Günter Grass (1927–); translated by Michael Hamburger

Chosen by Eleanor Bron

THE FOREST OF TANGLE

Deep in the Forest of Tangle
The King of the Makers sat
With a faggot of stripes for the tiger
And a flitter of wings for the bat.

He'd teeth and he'd claws for the cayman
And barks for the foxes and seals,
He'd a grindstone for sharpening swordfish
And electrical charges for eels.

He'd hundreds of kangaroo-pouches
On bushes and creepers and vines,
He'd hoots for the owls, and for glow-worms
He'd goodness knows how many shines.

He'd bellows for bullfrogs in dozens
And rattles for snakes by the score,
He'd hums for the humming-birds, buzzes for bees,
And elephant trumpets galore.

He'd pectoral fins for sea-fishes
With which they might glide through the air,
He'd porcupine quills and a bevy of bills
And various furs for the bear.

But O the old King of the Makers
With tears could have filled up a bay,
For no one had come to his warehouse
These many long years and a day.

And sadly the King of the Makers
His bits and his pieces he eyed
As he sat on a rock in the midst of his stock

And he cried and he cried and he cried.
He cried and he cried and he cried and he cried,
He cried and he cried and he cried.

Charles Causley (1917–)

Chosen by Brian Patten

It is a mysterious yet accessible poem of that rare kind that works equally
well for both children and adults and it is wonderful to read out loud.

THE SHEIKH WHO PLAYED WITH CHILDREN

A certain young man was asking around,
'I need to find a wise person. I have a problem.'

A bystander said, 'There's no one with intelligence
in our town except that man over there
playing with the children,
       the one riding the stick-horse.

He has keen, fiery insight and vast dignity
like the night sky, but he conceals it
in the madness of child's play.'

The young seeker approached the children, 'Dear father,
you who have become as a child, tell me a secret.'

'Go away. This is not a day
for secrets.'

      'But please! Ride your horse this way,
just for a minute.'

     The sheikh play-galloped over.
'Speak quickly. I can't hold this one still for long.
Whoops. Don't let him kick you.
        This is a wild one!'

The young man felt he couldn't ask his serious question
in the crazy atmosphere, so he joked,
        'I need to get married.
Is there someone suitable on this street?'

'There are three kinds of women in the world.
Two are griefs, and one is a treasure to the soul.

The first, when you marry her, is all yours.
The second is half-yours, and the third
is not yours at all.
                    Now get out of here,
before this horse kicks you in the head! Easy now!'

The sheikh rode off among the children.
The young man shouted, 'Tell me more about the kinds of
    women!'

The sheikh, on his cane horsie, came closer,
'The virgin of your first love is all yours.
She will make you feel happy and free. A childless widow
is the second. She will be half-yours. The third,
who is nothing to you, is a married woman with a child.
By her first husband she had a child, and all her love
goes into that child. She will have no connection with you.
Now watch out.
              Back away.
                        I'm going to turn this rascal around!'
He gave a loud whoop and rode back,
calling the children around him.

'One more question, Master!'
                          The sheikh circled,
'What is it? Quickly! That rider over there needs me.
I think I'm in love.'
                    'What is this playing that you do?
Why do you hide your intelligence so?'
                                        'The people here
want to put me in charge. They want me to be
judge, magistrate, and interpreter of all the texts.

The knowing I have doesn't want that. It wants to enjoy itself.
I am a plantation of sugarcane, and at the same time

I'm eating the sweetness.'
                              Knowledge that is acquired
is not like this. Those who have it worry if
audiences like it or not.
                              It's a bait for popularity.

Disputational knowing wants customers.
It has no soul.
                    Robust and energetic
before a responsive crowd, it slumps when no one is there.
The only real customer is God.

                    Chew quietly
your sweet sugarcane God-Love, and stay
playfully childish.
                    Your face
will turn rosy with illumination
like the redbud flowers.

~

Let the lover be disgraceful, crazy,
absentminded. Someone sober
will worry about things going badly.
Let the lover be.

~

All day and night, music,
a quiet, bright
reedsong. If it
fades, we fade.

Rumi (1207–73); translated by Coleman Barks

Chosen by Will Self

I chose 'The Sheikh Who Played with Children' for several reasons. Personally, because I went to the 527th Festival of the Mevlana in Konya in Turkey and was very moved. Also, Rumi is regarded as the Shakespeare of the Islamic world and it seems suitable to choose a poem by an author who is an integral part of the world view of Islamic people (many of whom are currently in the process of becoming refugees), but who is virtually unknown in the west. As for the poem itself, it is a beautiful evocation of the wisdom of the so-called 'drunken' Sufis, expressing a love of the divine that is simultaneously transcendent and immanent. It also has practical things to say of the life of the heart, the relationship between sanity and play, and in the final two stanzas it recapitulates a sense of the being of humans as phenomenon of being rather than having.

THE WINTER PALACE

Most people know more as they get older:
I give all that the cold shoulder.

I spent my second quarter-century
Losing what I had learnt at university

And refusing to take in what had happened since.
Now I know none of the names in the public prints,

And am starting to give offence by forgetting faces
And swearing I've never been in certain places.

It will be worth it, if in the end I manage
To blank out whatever it is that is doing the damage.

Then there will be nothing I know.
My mind will fold into itself, like fields, like snow.

Philip Larkin (1922–85)

Chosen by Bill Nighy

A BLADE OF GRASS

You ask for a poem.
I offer you a blade of grass.
You say it is not good enough.
You ask for a poem.

I say this blade of grass will do.
It has dressed itself in frost,
It is more immediate
Than any image of my making.

You say it is not a poem,
It is a blade of grass and grass
Is not quite good enough.
I offer you a blade of grass.

You are indignant.
You say it is too easy to offer grass.
It is absurd.
Anyone can offer a blade of grass.

You ask for a poem.
And so I write you a tragedy about
How a blade of grass
Becomes more and more difficult to offer,

And about how as you grow older
A blade of grass
Becomes more difficult to accept.

Brian Patten (1946–)

Chosen by Virginia McKenna

I'm a great fan of Brian Patten, and this poem brilliantly describes how complicated we all become, how convoluted our outlook on life. A frost-robed blade of grass must surely be one of the beauties of nature, but perhaps it takes an open and undemanding heart to recognise it.

FROM 'NIGHT THE SECOND', *VALA, OR THE FOUR ZOAS*

(The prophetic figure of Enion is wailing 'from the dark deep'.)

'What is the price of Experience? Do men buy it for a song?
Or wisdom for a dance in the street? No, it is bought with
the price
Of all that a man hath, his house, his wife, his children.
Wisdom is sold in the desolate market where none come to buy,
And in the withered field where the farmer ploughs for bread
in vain.

'It is an easy thing to triumph in the summer's sun
And in the vintage and to sing on the wagon loaded with corn
It is an easy thing to talk of patience to the afflicted,
To speak the laws of prudence to the houseless wanderer,
To listen to the hungry raven's cry in wintry season
When the red blood is fill'd with wine and with the marrow
of lambs.

It is an easy thing to laugh at wrathful elements,
To hear the dog howl at the wintry door, the ox in the slaughter
house moan:
To see a god on every wind and a blessing on every blast;
To hear sounds of love in the thunder storm that destroys our
enemies' house.
To rejoice in the blight that covers his field and the sickness that
cuts off his children.
While our olive and vine sing and laugh round our door, and our
children bring fruits and flowers.

Then the groan and the dolor are quite forgotten, and the slave
grinding at the mill,
And the captive in chains, and the poor in the prison, and the
soldier in the field

When the shatter'd bone hath laid him groaning among the
   happier dead.

It is an easy thing to rejoice in the tents of prosperity:
Thus could I sing and thus rejoice: but it is not so with me.'

William Blake (1757–1827)

Chosen by Jack Shepherd

It is exactly the sort of poem you don't want to say anything about. It's what
you feel when you get news of disaster, death, destruction and suffering
from distant places and you're in a warm, well-fed, comfortable situation.
The poem expresses that terrible contradiction.

   The reason I chose Blake is because reproductions of his paintings hung
on the walls of a Baptist Church I used to go to when I was little and at
first I was terrified of them, and then fascinated. When I grew up I became
completely involved in his paintings and writing – so much so that I wrote
a play about him.

EVERYONE SANG

Everyone suddenly burst out singing;
And I was filled with such delight
As prisoned birds must find in freedom
Winging wildly across the white
Orchards and dark-green fields; on; on; and out of sight.

Everyone's voice was suddenly lifted,
And beauty came like the setting sun.
My heart was shaken with tears; and horror
Drifted away . . . O but every one
Was a bird; and the song was wordless; the singing will never
  be done.

Siegfried Sassoon (1886–1967)

Chosen by Lord Woolf and by Patrick Allen

'Everyone Sang' is so exultantly, rapturously joyous that it cheers me and
lifts the spirit. I hope it will for others!

on love and loss

THE SUN HAS BURST THE SKY

The sun has burst the sky
Because I love you
And the river its banks.

The sea laps the great rocks
Because I love you
And takes no heed of the moon dragging it away
And saying coldly 'Constancy is not for you.'

The blackbird fills the air
Because I love you
With spring and lawns and shadows falling on lawns.

The people walk in the street and laugh
I love you
And far down the river ships sound their hooters
Crazy with joy because I love you.

Jenny Joseph (1932–)

Chosen by Helen Lederer

I am enchanted by this poem. It is uplifting, engaging and sweetly egocentric. It's about that feeling when one is overwhelmed by being in love. It convinces me that all the magnificent things in the world – like the sun and the sea and the birds – only exist because of being in love. Which is quite true – after all it always rains when one's just been dumped, doesn't it?

COLOURS

When your face
appeared over my crumpled life
at first I understood
only the poverty of what I have.
Then its particular light
on woods, on rivers, on the sea,
became my beginning in the coloured world
in which I had not yet had my beginning.
I am so frightened, I am so frightened,
of the unexpected sunrise finishing,
of revelations
and tears and the excitement finishing.
I don't fight it, my love is this fear,
I nourish it who can nourish nothing,
love's slipshod watchman.
Fear hems me in.
I am conscious that these minutes are short
and that the colours in my eyes will vanish
when your face sets.

Yevgeny Yevtushenko (1933 –); translated by
Robin Milner-Gulland and Peter Levi

Chosen by Martin Jarvis

DOVER BEACH

The sea is calm to-night.
The tide is full, the moon lies fair
Upon the straits; — on the French coast the light
Gleams and is gone; the cliffs of England stand,
Glimmering and vast, out in the tranquil bay.
Come to the window, sweet is the night-air!
Only, from the long line of spray
Where the sea meets the moon-blanch'd sand,
Listen! you hear the grating roar
Of pebbles which the waves suck back, and fling,
At their return, up the high strand,
Begin, and cease, and then again begin,
With tremulous cadence slow, and bring
The eternal note of sadness in.

Sophocles long ago
Heard it on the Aegean, and it brought
Into his mind the turbid ebb and flow
Of human misery; we
Find also in the sound a thought,
Hearing it by this distant northern sea.

The sea of faith
Was once, too, at the full, and round earth's shore
Lay like the folds of a bright girdle furl'd;
But now I only hear
Its melancholy, long, withdrawing roar,
Retreating to the breath
Of the night-wind, down the vast edges drear
And naked shingles of the world.

Ah, love, let us be true
To one another! for the world, which seems

To lie before us like a land of dreams,
So various, so beautiful, so new,
Hath really neither joy, nor love, nor light,
Nor certitude, nor peace, nor help for pain;
And we are here as on a darkling plain
Swept with confused alarms of struggle and flight,
Where ignorant armies clash by night.

Matthew Arnold (1822–88)

Chosen by Eileen Atkins

Since 'ignorant armies' are still 'clashing by night', I fear Matthew Arnold's poem will always be relevant, but he does also ask his love to be true to him and that question will always be relevant as well, and a true love of any kind for anyone or anything is probably the greatest thing that this life offers us.

WALKING AWAY

It is eighteen years ago, almost to the day –
A sunny day with the leaves just turning,
The touch-lines new-ruled – since I watched you play
Your first game of football, then, like a satellite
Wrenched from its orbit, go drifting away

Behind a scatter of boys. I can see
You walking away from me towards the school
With the pathos of a half-fledged thing set free
Into the wilderness, the gait of one
Who finds no path where the path should be.

That hesitant figure, eddying away
Like a winged seed loosened from its parent stem,
Has something I never quite grasp to convey
About nature's give-and-take – the small, the scorching
Ordeals which fire one's irresolute clay.

I have had worse partings, but none that so
Gnaws at my mind still. Perhaps it is roughly
Saying what God alone could perfectly show –
How selfhood begins with a walking away,
And love is proved in the letting go.

C. Day Lewis (1904–72)

Chosen by Geoffrey Palmer

I did not know this poem until I read it on *Woman's Hour* in a lovely selection
called 'Growing Pains', produced by Lindsay Leonard.

It needs no explanation – I just think it is quite beautiful.

FOR A FATHERLESS SON

You will be aware of an absence, presently,
Growing beside you, like a tree,
A death tree, colour gone, an Australian gum tree –
Balding, gelded by lightning – an illusion,
And a sky like a pig's backside, an utter lack of attention.

But right now you are dumb.
And I love your stupidity,
The blind mirror of it. I look in
And find no face but my own, and you think that's funny.
It is good for me

To have you grab my nose, a ladder rung.
One day you may touch what's wrong
The small skulls, the smashed blue hills, the godawful hush.
Till then your smiles are found money.

Sylvia Plath (1932–63)

Chosen by Nicholas Glass

A friend lost his elder brother in the second tower and that brother had
a young son. Plath's poem addresses someone too young to grasp the
'godawful' loss. But it has a hope, a tenderness about it: 'Your smiles are
found money.' And I love that.

142

ALL THINGS ARE QUITE SILENT

All things are quite silent, each mortal at rest,
When me and my love got snug in one nest,
When a bold set of ruffians they entered our cave,
And they forced my dear jewel to plough the salt wave.

I begged hard for my sailor as though I begged for life.
They'd not listen to me although a fond wife,
Saying: 'The king he wants sailors, to the sea he must go,'
And they've left me lamenting in sorrow and woe.

Through green fields and meadows we ofttimes did walk,
And sweet conversation of love we have talked,
With the birds in the woodland so sweetly did sing,
And the lovely thrushes' voices made the valleys to ring.

Although my love's gone I will not be cast down.
Who knows but my sailor may once more return?
And will make me amends for all trouble and strife,
And my true love and I might live happy for life.

Anon.

Chosen by Willy Russell

I chose this because although there are many many named poets whose work
I love, Anon has always been one of my favourites. 'All Things Are Quite
Silent' seems to be a particularly fine example of Anon's work.

ON THE TWELFTH DAY I SCREAMED

(A Letter from his Girl to a GI in Tokyo)

Now April's here, what ever can I do
With these fantastic gifts I got from you?
Spring's in the air, but honey, life is hard:
The three French hens are picking in the yard,
And the turtledove, the turtledove
(One of them died) –
Ah love, my own true love, you have denied
Me nothing the mails or the express could bring.
But look: we're into spring:
The calling birds are calling, calling:
The pear tree's leaves are slowly falling:
I sit here with those cackling geese
And never know a moment's peace.
My memories are mixed and hazy;
The drumming drummers drive me crazy,
The milking maids enjoy canasta,
The lords are leaping ever faster,
The pipers – God in Heaven knows
I've more than had enough of those.

My love, you do such wondrous things
(Who else would think of <u>five</u> gold rings?)
I know you send me all you can
Of spoils of occupied Japan,
But you remain on alien shore
And waiting here is such a bore.
My love, the lively lords are leaping:
Some things will not improve with keeping.

Now April's here, the weary days go by;
I watch that wretched dove attempt to fly;

The partridge smells; the geese are getting hoarse;
My diction's growing positively coarse.
You must forgive my gestures of rejection –
I'm crazed with all your tokens of affection.
Enough's enough; next time be less romantic
And don't send gifts that drive a lady frantic.
Send me a postcard with a pretty view
And I shall look at it and think of you.

David Daiches (1912–)

Chosen by Susan Hampshire

The wind was a torrent of darkness among the gusty trees,
The moon was a ghostly galleon tossed upon cloudy seas,
The road was a ribbon of moonlight over the purple moor,
And the highwayman came riding —
     Riding — riding —
The highwayman came riding, up to the old inn-door.

He'd a French cocked-hat on his forehead, a bunch of lace at
  his chin,
A coat of claret velvet, and breeches of brown doe-skin;
They fitted with never a wrinkle: his boots were up to the thigh!
And he rode with a jewelled twinkle,
     His pistol butts a-twinkle,
His rapier hilt a-twinkle, under the jewelled sky.

Over the cobbles he clattered and clashed in the dark inn-yard,
And he tapped with his whip on the shutters, but all was locked
  and barred;
He whistled a tune to the window, and who should be
  waiting there
But the landlord's black-eyed daughter,
     Bess, the landlord's daughter,
Plaiting a dark red love-knot into her long black hair.

And dark in the dark old inn-yard a stable-wicket creaked
Where Tim the ostler listened; his face was white and peaked;
His eyes were hollows of madness, his hair like mouldy hay,
But he loved the landlord's daughter,
     The landlord's red-lipped daughter;
Dumb as a dog he listened, and he heard the robber say —

'One kiss, my bonny sweetheart, I'm after a prize to-night,
But I shall be back with the yellow gold before the morning light;
Yet, if they press me sharply, and harry me through the day,
Then look for me by moonlight,
    Watch for me by moonlight,
I'll come to thee by moonlight, though hell should bar the way.'

He rose upright in the stirrups; he scarce could reach her hand,
But she loosened her hair i' the casement! His face burnt
  like a brand
As the black cascade of perfume came tumbling over his breast;
And he kissed its waves in the moonlight,
    (Oh, sweet black waves in the moonlight!)
Then he tugged at his rein in the moonlight, and galloped away to
  the west.

He did not come in the dawning; he did not come at noon;
And out o' the tawny sunset, before the rise o' the moon,
When the road was a gipsy's ribbon, looping the purple moor,
A red-coat troop came marching –
    Marching – marching –
King George's men came marching, up to the old inn-door.

They said no word to the landlord, they drank his ale instead,
But they gagged his daughter and bound her to the foot of her
  narrow bed;
Two of them knelt at her casement, with muskets at their side!
There was death at every window;
    And hell at one dark window;
For Bess could see, through her casement, the road that *he*
  would ride.
They had tied her up to attention, with many a sniggering jest;
They had bound a musket beside her, with the barrel beneath
  her breast!

'Now keep good watch!' and they kissed her.
　　She heard the dead man say –
Look for me by moonlight;
　　Watch for me by moonlight;
I'll come to thee by moonlight, though hell should bar the way!

She twisted her hands behind her; but all the knots held good!
She writhed her hands till her fingers were wet with sweat
　　or blood!
They stretched and strained in the darkness, and the hours crawled
　　by like years,
Till, now, on the stroke of midnight,
　　Cold, on the stroke of midnight,
The tip of one finger touched it! The trigger at least was hers!

The tip of one finger touched it; she strove no more for the rest!
Up, she stood to attention, with the barrel beneath her breast,
She would not risk their hearing; she would not strive again;
For the road lay bare in the moonlight;
　　Blank and bare in the moonlight;
And the blood of her veins in the moonlight throbbed to her
　　love's refrain.

Tlot-tlot; tlot-tlot! Had they heard it? The horse-hoofs ringing clear;
Tlot-tlot, tlot-tlot, in the distance? Were they deaf that they did
　　not hear?
Down the ribbon of moonlight, over the brow of the hill,
The highwayman came riding,
　　Riding, riding!
The red-coats looked to their priming! She stood up, straight
　　and still!

Tlot-tlot, in the frosty silence! *tlot-tlot,* in the echoing night!
Nearer he came and nearer! Her face was like a light!
Her eyes grew wide for a moment; she drew one last deep breath,

Then her finger moved in the moonlight,
      Her musket shattered the moonlight,
Shattered her breast in the moonlight and warned him — with
   her death.

He turned; he spurred to the westward; he did not know
   who stood
Bowed, with her head o'er the musket, drenched with her own
   red blood!
Not till the dawn he heard it, and slowly blanched to hear
How Bess, the landlord's daughter,
      The landlord's black-eyed daughter,
Had watched for her love in the moonlight, and died in the
   darkness there.

Back, he spurred like a madman, shrieking a curse to the sky,
With the white road smoking behind him and his rapier
   brandished high!
Blood-red were his spurs i' the golden noon; wine-red was his
   velvet coat;
When they shot him down on the highway,
      Down like a dog on the highway,
And he lay in his blood on the highway, with the bunch of lace at
   his throat.

And still of a winter's night, they say, when the wind is in the trees,
When the moon is a ghostly galleon tossed upon cloudy seas,
When the road is a ribbon of moonlight over the purple moor,
A highwayman comes riding
      Riding — riding —
A highwayman comes riding, up to the old inn-door.

Over the cobbles he clatters and clangs in the dark inn-yard
And he taps with his whip on the shutters, but all is locked and barred;
He whistles a tune to the window, and who should be waiting there

> *But the landlord's black-eyed daughter,*
> *Bess, the landlord's daughter,*
> *Plaiting a dark red love-knot into her long black hair.*

Alfred Noyes (1880–1959)

Chosen by Joanna Lumley

There are *many* different types of poetry – and one of the very oldest is Narrative Verse, which tells a story and is meant to be declaimed aloud to an audience. 'The Highwayman' is just that – there's a thrilling beat to the hoofs of the highwayman's horse; one can almost hear the stable door creaking as the jealous groom eavesdrops; the marching of King George's men coming dreadfully down the evening road. If I had to start young people falling in love with poetry, I'd start with this story of romance and heroism.

TO HIS COY MISTRESS

Had we but world enough, and time,
This coyness, Lady, were no crime
We would sit down and think which way
To walk and pass our long love's day.
Thou by the Indian Ganges' side
Should'st rubies find: I by the tide
Of Humber would complain. I would
Love you ten years before the Flood,
And you should, if you please, refuse
Till the conversion of the Jews.
My vegetable love should grow
Vaster than empires, and more slow.
An hundred years should go to praise
Thine eyes and on thy forehead gaze;
Two hundred to adore each breast,
But thirty thousand to the rest.
An age at least to every part,
And the last age should show your heart.
For, Lady, you deserve this state,
Nor would I love at lower rate.

But at my back I always hear
Time's wingèd chariot hurrying near;
And yonder all before us lie
Deserts of vast eternity.
Thy beauty shall no more be found,
Nor, in my marble vault, shall sound
My echoing song: then worms shall try
That long preserved virginity,
And your quaint honour turn to dust,
And into ashes all my lust.
The grave's a fine and private place,
But none, I think, do there embrace.

Now therefore, while the youthful hue

Sits on thy skin like morning dew,
And while thy willing soul transpires
At every pore with instant fires,
Now let us sport us while we may,
And now, like amorous birds of prey,
Rather at once our time devour
Than languish in his slow-chapt power.
Let us roll all our strength and all
Our sweetness up into one ball,
And tear our pleasures with rough strife
Through the iron gates of life:
Thus, though we cannot make our sun
Stand still, yet we will make him run.

Andrew Marvell (1621–78)

Chosen by Julian Clary

It made me laugh as a young boy and it still does in the oblique way it deals
with sex.

LUCY: SHE DWELT AMONG TH' UNTRODDEN WAYS

She dwelt among th' untrodden ways
    Beside the springs of Dove,
A Maid whom there were none to praise
    And very few to love:

A violet by a mossy stone
    Half hidden from the eye!
— Fair as a star, when only one
    Is shining in the sky.

She lived unknown, and few could know
    When Lucy ceased to be;
But she is in her grave, and oh,
    The difference to me!

William Wordsworth (1770–1850)

Chosen by Frank Skinner

I like the economical style of Wordsworth's writing in this poem. Every line bears close analysis. The last two lines say, in twelve words, all you need to know about loss.

AS I WALKED OUT ONE EVENING

As I walked out one evening,
　　Walking down Bristol Street,
The crowds upon the pavement
　　Were fields of harvest wheat.

And down by the brimming river
　　I heard a lover sing
Under an arch of the railway:
　　'Love has no ending.

'I'll love you, dear, I'll love you
　　Till China and Africa meet,
And the river jumps over the mountain
　　And the salmon sing in the street,

'I'll love you till the ocean
　　Is folded and hung up to dry
And the seven stars go squawking
　　Like geese about the sky.

'The years shall run like rabbits,
　　For in my arms I hold
The Flower of the Ages,
　　And the first love of the world.'

But all the clocks in the city
　　Began to whirr and chime:
'O let not Time deceive you,
　　You cannot conquer Time.

'In the burrows of the Nightmare
　　Where Justice naked is,

Time watches from the shadow
　And coughs when you would kiss.

'In headaches and in worry
　Vaguely life leaks away,
And Time will have his fancy
　To-morrow or to-day.

'Into many a green valley
　Drifts the appalling snow;
Time breaks the threaded dances
　And the diver's brilliant bow.

'O plunge your hands in water,
　Plunge them in up to the wrist;
Stare, stare in the basin
　And wonder what you've missed.

'The glacier knocks in the cupboard,
　The desert sighs in the bed,
And the crack in the tea-cup opens
　A lane to the land of the dead.

'Where the beggars raffle the banknotes
　And the Giant is enchanting to Jack,
And the Lily-white Boy is a Roarer,
　And Jill goes down on her back.

'O look, look in the mirror,
　O look in your distress;
Life remains a blessing
　Although you cannot bless.

'O stand, stand at the window
　As the tears scald and start;

You shall love your crooked neighbour
With your crooked heart.'

It was late, late in the evening,
    The lovers they were gone;
The clocks had ceased their chiming
    And the deep river ran on.

W. H. Auden (1907–73)

Chosen by Helen Fielding

SUDDENLY, THE FACE OF THE WORLD GROWS DIM

Suddenly, the face of the world grows dim
The Beloved appears from behind his veil
how my heart shivers and burns for him!
All the nine heavens shine sad with love.

Rumi (1207–73); translated by Coleman Barks

Chosen by Sean Hughes

Simplicity can break down the most complicated of emotions.

YOUR LAUGHTER

Take bread away from me, if you wish,
take air away, but
do not take from me your laughter.

Do not take away the rose,
the lanceflower that you pluck,
the water that suddenly
bursts forth in your joy,
the sudden wave
of silver born in you.

My struggle is harsh and I come back
with eyes tired
at times from having seen
the unchanging earth,
but when your laughter enters
it rises to the sky seeking me
and it opens for me all
the doors of life.

My love, in the darkest
hour your laughter
opens, and if suddenly
you see my blood staining
the stones of the street,
laugh, because your laughter
will be for my hands
like a fresh sword.

Next to the sea in the autumn,
your laughter must raise
its foamy cascade,
and in spring, love,

I want your laughter like
the flower I was waiting for,
the blue flower, the rose
of my echoing country.

Laugh at the night,
at the day, at the moon,
laugh at the twisted
streets of the island,
laugh at this clumsy
boy who loves you,
but when I open
my eyes and close them,
when my steps go,
when my steps return,
deny me bread, air,
light, spring,
but never your laughter
for I would die.

Pablo Neruda (1904–73); translated by Donald D. Walsh

Chosen by Martin Clunes

I will always love this poem. It was read at my wedding.

HE WISHES FOR THE CLOTHS OF HEAVEN

Had I the heavens' embroidered cloths,
Enwrought with golden and silver light,
The blue and the dim and the dark cloths
Of night and light and the half-light,
I would spread the cloths under your feet:
But I, being poor, have only my dreams;
I have spread my dreams under your feet;
Tread softly because you tread on my dreams.

W. B. Yeats (1865–1939)

Chosen by Fiona Shaw

'Cloths of Heaven' is quite simply one of the most perfect poems – all
imagination and all heart.

on nature

SPRING

Green-shadowed people sit, or walk in rings,
Their children finger the awakened grass,
Calmly a cloud stands, calmly a bird sings,
And, flashing like a dangled looking-glass,
Sun lights the balls that bounce, the dogs that bark,
The branch-arrested mist of leaf, and me,
Threading my pursed-up way across the park,
An indigestible sterility.

Spring, of all seasons most gratuitous,
Is fold of untaught flower, is race of water,
Is earth's most multiple, excited daughter;

And those she has least use for see her best,
Their paths grown craven and circuitous,
Their visions mountain-clear, their needs immodest.

Philip Larkin (1922–85)

Chosen by Julia MacKenzie

TO AUTUMN

Season of mists and mellow fruitfulness,
  Close bosom-friend of the maturing sun;
Conspiring with him how to load and bless
  With fruit the vines that round the thatch-eaves run;
To bend with apples the mossed cottage-trees,
  And fill all fruit with ripeness to the core;
    To swell the gourd, and plump the hazel shells
  With a sweet kernel; to set budding more,
And still more, later flowers for the bees,
Until they think warm days will never cease,
    For Summer has o'er-brimmed their clammy cells.

Who hath not seen thee oft amid thy store?
  Sometimes whoever seeks abroad may find
Thee sitting careless on a granary floor,
  Thy hair soft-lifted by the winnowing wind;
Or on a half-reaped furrow sound asleep,
  Drowsed with the fume of poppies, while thy hook
    Spares the next swath and all its twinèd flowers:
  And sometimes like a gleaner thou dost keep
Steady thy laden head across a brook;
Or by a cider-press, with patient look,
    Thou watchest the last oozings, hours by hours.

Where are the songs of Spring? Ay, where are they?
  Think not of them, thou hast thy music too –
While barrèd clouds bloom the soft-dying day,
  And touch the stubble-plains with rosy hue;
Then in a wailful choir the small gnats mourn
  Among the river sallows, borne aloft
    Or sinking as the light wind lives or dies;
  And full-grown lambs loud bleat from hilly bourn;
Hedge-crickets sing; and now with treble soft

The red-breast whistles from a garden croft;
And gathering swallows twitter in the skies.

John Keats (1795–1821)

Chosen by Christopher Cazenove

THE WINDHOVER

I caught this morning morning's minion, kingdom of daylight's
   dauphin,
      dapple-dawn-drawn Falcon, in his riding
Of the rolling level underneath him steady air, and striding
High there, how he rung upon the rein of a wimpling wing
In his ecstasy! then off, off forth on swing,
As a skate's heel sweeps smooth on a bow-bend: the hurl
   and gliding
Rebuffed the big wind. My heart in hiding
Stirred for a bird, – the achieve of, the mastery of the thing!

Brute beauty and valour and act, oh, air, pride, plume, here
Buckle! and the fire that breaks from thee then, a billion
Times told lovelier, more dangerous, O my chevalier!

No wonder of it: shéer plód makes plough down sillion
Shine, and blue-bleak embers, ah my dear,
Fall, gall themselves, and gash gold-vermilion.

Gerard Manley Hopkins (1844–89)

Chosen by Anthony Hooper

I have chosen this piece because it has been my favourite poem since I first
read it some fifty years ago. The various species of falcon have now made
a big recovery in this country following the outlawing of the poison DDT
and the taking of other steps to protect them and to increase their numbers.
On journeys down a motorway many kestrels may be seen hunting the verges
on either side of road. We can help to protect them, we can sometimes tame
them through the art of falconry but we can never master them. Remember
this poem when next you see one!

SNAKE

A snake came to my water-trough
On a hot, hot day, and I in pyjamas for the heat,
To drink there.

In the deep, strange-scented shade of the great dark carob-tree
I came down the steps with my pitcher
And must wait, must stand and wait, for there he was at the trough
  before me.

He reached down from a fissure in the earth-wall in the gloom
And trailed his yellow-brown slackness soft-bellied down, over the
  edge of the stone trough
And rested his throat upon the stone bottom,
And where the water had dripped from the tap, in a small clearness,
He sipped with his straight mouth,
Softly drank through his straight gums, into his slack long body,
Silently.

Someone was before me at my water-trough,
And I, like a second comer, waiting.

He lifted his head from his drinking, as cattle do,
And looked at me vaguely, as drinking cattle do,
And flickered his two-forked tongue from his lips, and mused a
  moment,
And stooped and drank a little more,
Being earth-brown, earth-golden from the burning bowels of
  the earth
On the day of Sicilian July, with Etna smoking.

The voice of my education said to me
He must be killed,
For in Sicily the black, black snakes are innocent, the gold are
  venomous.

And voices in me said, If you were a man
You would take a stick and break him now, and finish him off.
But must I confess how I liked him,
How glad I was he had come like a guest in quiet, to drink at my
    water-trough
And depart peaceful, pacified, and thankless,
Into the burning bowels of this earth?

Was it cowardice, that I dared not kill him?
Was it perversity, that I longed to talk to him?
Was it humility, to feel so honoured?
I felt so honoured.

And yet those voices:
If you were not afraid, you would kill him!

And truly I was afraid, I was most afraid,
But even so, honoured still more
That he should seek my hospitality
From out the dark door of the secret earth.

He drank enough
And lifted his head, dreamily, as one who has drunken,
And flickered his tongue like a forked night on the air, so black,
Seeming to lick his lips,
And looked around like a god, unseeing, into the air,
And slowly turned his head,
And slowly, very slowly, as if thrice adream,
Proceeded to draw his slow length curving round
And climb again the broken bank of my wall-face.

And as he put his head into that dreadful hole,
And as he slowly drew up, snake-easing his shoulders, and
    entered farther,
A sort of horror, a sort of protest against his withdrawing into that
    horrid black hole,

Deliberately going into the blackness, and slowly drawing
   himself after,
Overcame me now his back was turned.
I looked round, I put down my pitcher,
I picked up a clumsy log
And threw it at the water-trough with a clatter.

I think it did not hit him,
But suddenly that part of him that was left behind convulsed in
   undignified haste,
Writhed like lightning, and was gone
Into the black hole, the earth-lipped fissure in the wall-front,
At which, in the intense still noon, I stared with fascination.

And immediately I regretted it.
I thought how paltry, how vulgar, what a mean act!
I despised myself and the voices of my accursed human education.

And I thought of the albatross
And I wished he would come back, my snake.

For he seemed to me again like a king,
Like a king in exile, uncrowned in the underworld,
Now due to be crowned again.

And so, I missed my chance with one of the lords
Of life.
And I have something to expiate:
A pettiness.

D. H. Lawrence (1885–1930)

Chosen by Penelope Wilton

PIED BEAUTY

Glory be to God for dappled things –
For skies of couple-colour as a brinded cow;
　　For rose-moles all in stipple upon trout that swim;
Fresh fire-coal chestnut-falls; finches' wings;
　　Landscape plotted and pieced – fold, fallow, and plough;
　　　And all trades, their gear and tackle and trim.

All things counter, original, spare, strange;
　　Whatever is fickle, freckled (who knows how?)
With swift, slow; sweet, sour; adazzle, dim;
　　He fathers-forth whose beauty is past change:
　　　Praise him.

Gerard Manley Hopkins (1844–89)

Chosen by Prunella Scales

THE TREES

The trees are coming into leaf
Like something almost being said;
The recent buds relax and spread,
Their greenness is a kind of grief.

Is it that they are born again
And we grow old? No, they die too.
Their yearly trick of looking new
Is written down in rings of grain.

Yet still the unresting castles thresh
In fullgrown thickness every May.
Last year is dead, they seem to say,
Begin afresh, afresh, afresh.

Philip Larkin (1922–85)

Chosen by Tom Stoppard

It's one of my favourite poems by one of my favourite poets.

on hope

GRIEF

Grief ought to be used
To create more love;
There's no greater force
From below or above.

Such grief as we have seen
Could water the roots
Of a new world dream.
Give the dead the power

To change the world
Into something higher;
That we may listen to hunger's
Cry and turn injustice into a flower.

This is the strange blessing
Of those flaming towers:
That we may wake up to world suffering
And with vision sweeten humanity's hours.

Ben Okri, 2001

Human beings suffer,
They torture one another,
They get hurt and get hard.
No poem or play or song
Can fully right a wrong
Inflicted and endured.

The innocent in gaols
Beat on their bars together.
A hunger-striker's father
Stands in the graveyard dumb.
The police widow in veils
Faints at the funeral home.

History says, *Don't hope
On this side of the grave.*
But then, once in a lifetime
The longed-for tidal wave
Of justice can rise up,
And hope and history rhyme.

So hope for a great sea-change
On the far side of revenge.
Believe that a further shore
Is reachable from here.
Believe in miracles
And cures and healing wells.

Call miracle self-healing:
The utter, self-revealing
Double-take of feeling.

If there's fire on the mountain
Or lightning and storm
And a god speaks from the sky

That means someone is hearing
The outcry and the birth-cry
Of new life at its term.

Seamus Heaney (1939–)

Chosen by Jon Snow

I have chosen an extract from Seamus Heaney's *The Cure at Troy*. A brilliant
and uplifting poem about how great good can arise from great evil. I refer
to it much; it informs my optimistic view of life which I must confess has
taken a battering of late.

ANTHEM

The birds they sang
at the break of day
Start again,
I heard them say,
Don't dwell on what
has passed away
or what is yet to be.

The wars they will
be fought again
The holy dove
be caught again
bought and sold
and bought again;
the dove is never free

Ring the bells that still can ring.
Forget your perfect offering.
There is a crack in everything.
That's how the light gets in.

We asked for signs
the signs were sent:
the birth betrayed,
the marriage spent;
the widowhood
of every government –
signs for all to see.

Can't run no more
with that lawless crowd
while the killers in high places
say their prayers out loud.

But they've summoned up
a thundercloud
They're going to hear from me.

Ring the bells that still can ring.
Forget your perfect offering.
There is a crack in everything.
That's how the light gets in.

You can add up the parts
but you won't have the sum
You can strike up the march,
There is no drum.
Every heart
to love will come
but like a refugee.

Ring the bells that still can ring.
Forget your perfect offering.
There is a crack in everything.
That's how the light gets in.

Leonard Cohen (1934–)

Chosen by Bono

Holy Smoke. Leonard Cohen's voice on this one is Incense . . . part offering, part noxious, a strong scent getting up the nose of anyone who might stray into the contradictions of Religion. God. The idea that all of us are equal is a central tenet to Christianity, but we don't really believe it . . . do we?

Not of Jews. Not of Women. Not of Africans. Not of Moslems. Not of Buddhists. Not of Hindus – there's too many of them . . . and they're too far away for us to share their grief, when their houses and their lives evaporate before our TV dinner eyes. Deep down, we think they're not worth as much as us. Really. Neither God or History will let us get away with this . . .

But back to the poet and his big baritone sliding down to bass, like the drunken arm of a trombone player . . . 'Bella Lugosi Canto' I call it. I can still hear this voice when I read these words. I have chosen them though, because these words stand up on their own. They stand up for comedy and the right to be ridiculous, as much as they stand up for dignity and the right to live like a human – Human Rights. They stand up for 'humanness'. The voice cracks 'that's how the light gets in'.

I heard a story that in the days following September 11th, New Yorkers jammed the switchboards of TV stations with the request not to round out the numbers of people who lost their lives on that day. Be specific was the message.

Each death had a life behind it and many around it . . . The demand was adhered to across the United States and Europe. That's no small victory. I just wish we could be bigger, big enough to take in the whole world . . . like the voice of Leonard Cohen.

REVENGE

My personal revenge will be your children's
right to schooling and to flowers.
My personal revenge will be this song
bursting for you with no more fears.
My personal revenge will be to make you see
the goodness in my people's eyes,
implacable in combat always
generous and firm in victory.

My personal revenge will be to greet you
'Good morning!' in streets with no beggars,
when instead of locking you inside
they say, 'Don't look so sad'
When you, the torturer,
daren't lift your head.
My personal revenge will be to give you
these hands you once ill-treated
with all their tenderness intact.

Luis Enrique Mejía Godoy (1945–); translated by Dinah Livingstone

*Song based on words by Tomás Borge addressed to his jailers and torturers.
After the triumph of the Nicaraguan Revolution in 1979, Tomás Borge
became Minister for the Interior and, famously, had his revenge by for-
giving them.*

Chosen by Harriet Walter

I first heard this poem read as part of an anthology performed in aid of
the Medical Foundation for the Care of Victims of Torture. That a person
could keep such sanity, such perspective and humane purpose alive in

the midst of horror and hatred is testament to the best of our human potential.

This poem is an aspiration shared by more people than we get to hear about. But it is not woolly wishful thinking from a comfy armchair. It comes from the front line.

THE BRIGHT FIELD

I have seen the sun break through
to illuminate a small field
for a while, and gone my way
and forgotten it. But that was the pearl
of great price, the one field that had
the treasure in it. I realise now
that I must give all that I have
to possess it. Life is not hurrying

on to a receding future, nor hankering after
an imagined past. It is the turning
aside like Moses to the Miracle
of the lit bush, to a brightness
that seemed as transitory as your youth
once, but is the eternity that awaits you.

R. S. Thomas (1913–2000)

Chosen by Jeanette Winterson

I love this poem — not forward, not back, but towards the burning bush
seems the way we need to go.

WILLIAM BLAKE SAYS: EVERY THING THAT LIVES IS HOLY

Long live the Child
Long live the Mother and Father
Long live the People

Long live this wounded Planet
Long live the good milk of the Air
Long live the spawning Rivers and the
mothering Oceans
Long live the juice of the Grass
and all the determined greenery of the Globe

Long live the Elephants and the Sea Horses,
the Humming-Birds and the Gorillas,
the Dogs and Cats and Field-Mice —
all the surviving Animals
our innocent Sisters and Brothers

Long live the Earth, deeper than all our thinking

we have done enough killing

Long live the Man
Long live the Woman
Who use both courage and compassion
Long live their Children

Adrian Mitchell, 2001

on faith

A SONG ABOUT A DONKEY

The following is about the dangers
of imitating others in your spiritual life.

Meet the Friend on your own.
Try to dissolve out of selfishness
into a voice beyond those limits.

A wandering sufi came with his donkey
to a community of sufis who were very poor.
He fed the donkey and gave it water,
left it with his servant, and went inside.

Immediately, a group of the resident sufis
sold the donkey and bought food and candles
for a feast.
                    There was jubilation in the monastery!
No more patience and three-day fasting!

If you are rich and full-fed, don't laugh
at the impulsiveness of the poor.
They were not acting from their souls,
but they were acting out of some necessity.

The traveller joined in the festivities.
They paid constant attention to him,
caressing him, honouring him.
                                The *sema* began.
There was smoke from the kitchen,
dust from the feet hitting the floor,
and ecstasy from the longing of the dancers.

Their hands were waving.
Their foreheads swept low across the dais.
It had been a long wait for such an occasion.

Sufis always have to wait a long time
for their desire. That's why they're such
great eaters!
    The sufi who feeds on light, though,
is different, but there's only one of those
in a thousand. The rest live under
that one's protection.
      The *sema* ran its course
and ended. The poet began to sing a deep grief song,
'The donkey is gone, my son. Your donkey is gone.'

Everyone joined in, clapping their hands and singing
over and over, 'The donkey is gone, my son.
Your donkey is gone.'
     And the visiting sufi
sang more passionately than all the rest. Finally,
it was dawn, and they parted with many good-byes.
The banquet room was empty. The man brought out
his baggage and called to his servant,
'Where's my donkey?'
       'Look at you!'
         'What do you mean?'
'They sold your donkey! That's how we had
such a celebration!'
       'Why didn't you come and tell me?'
'Several times I came near, but you were always
singing so loudly, "The donkey's gone,
the donkey's gone," that I thought you knew.
I thought you had a secret insight.'
       'Yes.
It was my imitation of their joy that caused this.'

Even the good delight of friends is at first
a reflection in you. Stay with them
until it becomes a realisation.
                                    The imitation here
came from the man's desire to be honoured.
It deafened him to what was being
so constantly said.

Remember there's only one reason
to do anything: a meeting with the Friend
is the only real payment.

Rumi (1207–73); translated by Coleman Barks

Chosen by John Cleese

I chose this poem firstly because the Persian mystic and poet Rumi was
born in what is now called Afghanistan. Secondly, it's about an approach
to religion that seems to me to be more valuable than fundamentalism.

O GOD OF EARTH AND ALTAR

O God of earth and altar,
Bow down and hear our cry,
Our earthly rulers falter,
Our people drift and die;
The walls of gold entomb us,
The swords of scorn divide,
Take not thy thunder from us,
But take away our pride.

From all that terror teaches,
From lies of tongue and pen,
From all the easy speeches
That comfort cruel men,
From sale and profanation
Of honour and the sword,
From sleep and from damnation,
Deliver us, good Lord.

Tie in a living tether
The prince and priest and thrall,
Bind all our lives together,
Smite us and save us all;
In ire and exultation
Aflame with faith, and free,
Lift up a living nation,
A single sword to thee.

G. K. Chesterton (1874–1936)

Chosen by Kit Hesketh-Harvey and Kate Rabett

Kit used to sing this hymn when he was a chorister at Canterbury Cathedral.
He chose it because the last line always made him cry.

FROM ST PAUL'S LETTER
TO THE PHILIPPIANS

Whatsoever things are true,
Whatsoever things are honest,
Whatsoever things are just,
Whatsoever things are pure,
Whatsoever things are lovely,
Whatsoever things are of good report;
If there be any virtue,
And if there be any praise,
Think on these things.

St Paul

Chosen by Donald Sinden

It is good that, at this time, we reflect on these things.

THE PRAYER OF ST FRANCIS

Lord, make me an instrument of thy peace.
Where there is hatred, let me sow love.
Where there is injury, pardon.
Where there is discord, unity.
Where there is doubt, faith.

Where there is error, truth.
Where there is despair, hope.
Where there is sadness, joy.
Where there is darkness, light.

Oh divine master, grant that I may not
so much seek to be consoled, as to console;
to be understood, as to understand;
to be loved, as to love.

For it is in giving that we receive,
it is in pardoning that we are pardoned,
it is in dying that we are born to eternal life.

St Francis

Chosen by David Suchet

A QUESTION TO ANY ARCHBISHOP

'Excuse me, Archbishop, but has Christ risen?'
'Why, yes. Christ is risen from the dead.'
'But is he really risen? Is he? If he is tell the people!
And we don't want your evidence,
We want your faith, spoken with conviction.
Take that man off the Cross,
And show us a vision of the Risen Man,
Strong and healthy with his sleeves rolled up,
And a blue-print of the Kingdom of God in his hands.'

Duncan McCowen (1900–69)

Chosen by Alec McCowen

This poem reminds me of my father's fascination with religion. He was an extremely religious man. He was also dazzlingly irreverent. He spoke of Jesus as a personal friend. He was always expecting him to appear as the Mystery Guest on the TV programme *What's My Line?* And once, when an unknown lady appeared, my father said, 'Perhaps it's Mrs Jesus!'

This poem combines his great faith and a little of his humour.

CHRIST THE PROPHET WITH THE
LIFE-GIVING HAND

I hear that Christ, the Prophet with the life-giving hand will come;
In these modern times, dressed he will be in his old, old way.
The cross and the hanging rope will rise from the courts of
   lies, thus;
And in every story, every fiction,
Lies will be painted in the hues of abuse;
And drenched in blood will be the sound of beauty and the voice
   of Truth.
And even friends will fail to confess their friendship and turn their
   faces away.
The wealth of loyalty of the heart will be weighed in coins
   of silver,
The winds will carry the dagger of tyranny and the stems of flowers
   will be covered in Blood
And filled with evil will be the earth that we live on.
The Messenger of God will be seen hanging from the cross,
And like swooning storm clouds will dance the blackness of society.
And even the shining goblet of the sun will appear totally black.
It is heard that Christ will be born again, and His birth will be
   rejoiced,
And from the crucifix of tyranny will descend the corpse of Christ
And shining on land and sea will be the truth of Christ.
The search for the broken-hearted followers of Christ will advance,
And the eyes of the blind will be filled with the light of Truth,
This beautiful and heart-entrancing, attractive
And strong light will come from Christ,
Mohammed, and Moses, and Abraham.

Ali Sardar Jafri, (1913–2000); translated and chosen by Saeed Jaffrey

The reason I chose this particular poem was to prove to non-believers how important Christ is to the Muslim religion; how much he is revered, loved and respected. He is remembered as the Prophet with the healing hand, or 'the life-giving hand'. Also, the late Ali Sardar Jafri was one of the great Urdu poets of the last century. Not only that, he was a close friend of mine. We first met in the early seventies on the fifth floor of Bush House, from where I used to not only act in plays but also write and narrate scripts in Urdu, Hindi and English for BBC's World Service Radio. A happy time and a happy meeting.

IN THE OPEN

Move into the clear.
Keep still, take your stand
Out in the place of fear
On the bare sand;

Where you have never been,
Where the small heart is chilled;
Where a small thing is seen,
And can be killed.

Under the open day,
So weak and so appalled,
Look up and try to say,
Here I am, for you called.

You must haunt the thin cover
By that awful place,
Till you can get it over
And look up into that face.

Ruth Pitter (1872–1992)

Chosen by Jenny Joseph

I don't think this poem needs any advocacy from me. Once it is before your
eyes and in your ears you will understand why I have chosen it.

A DROP OF UNCLOUDED BLOOD

All day I will think of these cities floating fragile
across the earth's crust
and of how they are in need
of a drop of magic blood
a drop of unclouded blood

All day I will think of snow and the small
violets like a giant's blood
splashed at random on the earth
All day I will stroll about hoping
for a drop of unclouded blood
to fall into my veins

I need my body to move loose through the world
Need my fingers to touch the skin
of children adrift in their temporary world
Beneath their dreaming is a drop of blood
refusing the sun's heat
a drop of blood more pure than any other blood

I need to walk through the pale light
that occupies the world
and believe it when a drop of blood says
Listen,
paradise is never far away
and simpler than you think it

I need to sever all connection with the habits
that make the heart
love only certain things
I need a drop of magic blood for that
a drop of unclouded blood

Brian Patten (1946–)

Chosen by Sophie Thompson

I find that often I love a poem but I don't really know why. I felt that about this poem years ago. After September 11th I came upon the poem again. I loved it even more. Now I think I know why.

on peace

FROM
THE TENT

Listen to presences inside poems,
Let them take you where they will.

Follow those private hints,
and never leave the premises.

Rumi (1207–73); translated by Coleman Barks

Chosen by Stephen Dillane

MORNING STAR

When you have
When you have
Little bit
Little bit
Of clear morning
Of clear sky
Try to catch
Try to catch
Your morning star

Josef Lebeck

Chosen by Robert Daws and Amanda Waring

A homeless, unknown poet, selling his works on the streets of Prague, wrote this poem. Its simple optimism somehow felt appropriate.

OF THE TERRIBLE DOUBT OF APPEARANCES

Of the terrible doubt of appearances,
Of the uncertainty after all – that we may be deluded,
That may-be reliance and hope are but speculations after all,
That may-be identity beyond the grave is a beautiful fable only,
May-be the things I perceive – the animals, plants, men, hills,
    shining and flowing waters
The skies of day and night – colors, densities, forms – May-be
    these are (as doubtless they are) only apparitions, and the real
    something has yet to be known;
(How often they dart out of themselves, as if to confound me and
    mock me!
How often I think neither I know, nor any man knows, aught
    of them;)
May-be seeming to me what they are (as doubtless they indeed but
    seem,) as from my present point of view – And might prove, (as
    of course they would,) naught of what they appear, or naught
    anyhow, from entirely changed points of view;
– To me, these, and the like of these, are curiously answer'd by my
    lovers, my dear friends,
When he whom I love travels with me, or sits a long while holding
    me by the hand,
When the subtle air, the impalpable, the sense that words and
    reason hold not, surround us and pervade us,
Then I am charged with untold and untellable wisdom – I am silent
    – I require nothing further,
I cannot answer the question of appearances, or that of identity
    beyond the grave;
But I walk or sit indifferent – I am satisfied,
He ahold of my hand has completely satisfied me.

Walt Whitman (1819–92)

Chosen by J. K. Rowling

FROM LITTLE GIDDING

We shall not cease from exploration
And the end of all our exploring
Will be to arrive where we started
And know the place for the first time.
Through the unknown, remembered gate
When the last of earth left to discover
Is that which was the beginning;
At the source of the longest river
The voice of the hidden waterfall
And the children in the apple-tree
Not known, because not looked for
But heard, half-heard, in the stillness
Between two waves of the sea.
Quick now, here, now, always –
A condition of complete simplicity
(Costing not less than everything)
And all shall be well and
All manner of thing shall be well
When the tongues of flame are in-folded
Into the crowned knot of fire
And the fire and the rose are one.

T. S. Eliot (1885–1965)

Chosen by the Editor

ONLY BREATH

Not Christian or Jew or Muslim, not Hindu,
Buddhist, sufi, or zen. Not any religion

or cultural system. I am not from the East
or the West, not out of the ocean or up

from the ground, not natural or ethereal, not
composed of elements at all. I do not exist,

am not an entity in this world or the next,
did not descend from Adam and Eve or any

origin story. My place is placeless, a trace
of the traceless. Neither body or soul.

I belong to the beloved, have seen the two
worlds as one and that one call to and know,

first, last, outer, inner, only that
breath breathing human being.

*   *   *

There is a way between voice and presence
where information flows.

In disciplined silence it opens.
With wandering talk it closes.

Rumi (1207–73); translated by Coleman Barks

Chosen by Nick Danziger

With thanks to the following for their invaluable help and support:

The Poetry Library, the Poetry Society, Sandy Hardy and Sudbourne School Brixton, Martin Jarvis, Kate Rabett and Kit Hesketh-Harvey, Panos Pictures, John Hegley, Nicholas Glass, Julia Barrie, Julie Taylor, Caroline Muir, David Calder, Dulwich Books, Amanda Waring, Kate Lynn Evans, Gudren Claire, Charlie Sidgewick, Una de Wet, I.C.M., Rebecca Carter, Jonathan Butler, Marcella Edwards, Stephen Parker, everyone at War Child, Ruth Owen and all my friends and family for their enthusiasm and patience.

ACKNOWLEDGEMENTS

I would like to thank the following for their patient help and generosity in granting me permission to reproduce the following copyright material:

Wendy Cope for 'Spared' © Wendy Cope 2001.

Faber and Faber Ltd. for 'September 1, 1939', 'Musée des Beaux Arts', 'Epitaph on a Tyrant' by W.H. Auden from *The English Auden*.

David Higham Associates for 'The News-Reel' by Louis MacNeice from *Collected Poems 1925–1948* published by Faber and Faber Ltd.

Black Sparrow Press for 'War' Copyright © 1992 by Charles Bukowski, from *The Last Night of the Earth Poems*.

Michael Rosen for 'How shall we defeat The Enemy?' © Michael Rosen 2001.

Faber and Faber Ltd. for 'When Statesmen Gravely Say' by W.H. Auden from *Shorts – Collected Shorter Poems 1927–1957*.

A.P. Watt Ltd. on behalf of Michael B.Yeats for 'He Wishes for the Cloths of Heaven' and 'The Second Coming' by W.B. Yeats from *The Collected Poems of W.B. Yeats*.

The estate of C.P. Cavafy and The Random House Group Ltd. for 'Waiting for the Barbarians' from *The Collected Poems* by C.P. Cavafy, translated by Edmund Keeley and Philip Sherrard, edited by George Savidas, published by the Hogarth Press.

James Fenton for his poems 'Wind' from *The Memory of War and Children in Exile Poems 1968–1983* published by King Penguin 1983 and 'The Ballad of the Shrieking Man' from *Out of Danger* published by Penguin 1993.

Methuen Publishing Ltd. for 'Song' *from* Mother Courage by Bertolt Brecht translated by W.H. Auden.

Tony Harrison and Gordon Dickerson for 'Species Barrier' © Tony Harrison 2001.

Mrs Howard Nemerov for 'The End of the War' by Howard Nemerov.

Methuen Publishing Ltd. for 'Motto', translated by John Willett and 'Concerning the Label Emigrant', translated by Stephen Spender from Bertolt Brecht *Poems 1913–1956*, edited by John Willet and Ralph Manheim, published by Methuen.

Anvil Press for 'The Survivor' by Tadeusz Rozewicz from *Tadeusz Rozewicz: They Came to See a Poet* translated by Adam Czerniawski, published by Anvil Press Poetry 1991.

Andrew Motion for 'The Voices Live' © Andrew Motion 2001.

Roger McGough for his poem 'Defying Gravity' from *Defying Gravity* published by Penguin 1993.

Faber and Faber Ltd. for 'A Clear Day and No Memories' by Wallace Stevens from *Opus Posthumous* published by Faber and Faber Ltd 1990.

Carcanet Press Ltd. for 'The Departure Lounge' by Adam Johnson from *The Playground Bell* published by Carcanet Press Ltd. 1994, edited by Neil Powell.

Jenny Secombe and the family of the late Sir Harry Secombe for his poem 'Growing Older' © Jenny Secombe 2002.

of Exile' by Bertolt Brecht, from *Versions* published by Odyssey Poets 1999.

Sophie's Silver Lining Fund for 'On Being Alone at a Railway Station' by Sophie Large from *Sophie's Log* published by Sophie's Silver Lining Fund 1999.

Lotte Kramer for 'Boy With Orange' from *The Phantom Lane* Rockingham Press 2000.

Rockingham Press for 'The Embrace' by Oktay Rifat from *Voices of Memory: Selected Poems of Oktay Rifat*, Rockingham Press 1993 translated by Ruth Christie.

Vikram Seth for 'All You Who Sleep Tonight' © Vikram Seth 1990.

Time Warner Books U.K. for 'Human Family' by Maya Angelou from *I Shall Not be Moved* published by Virago Press 1990, first published in the USA and Canada by Random House, 1990.

Fay Hart for her poem 'When I was in China' © Fay Hart 2002.

Tom Leonard for his poem 'Unrelated Incidents (3)' from *Intimate Voices 1965–1983* published by Galloping Dog Press 1984.

John Hegley and Carlton Publishing Group for 'Photo in St James' Park' by John Hegley from *Glad to Wear Glasses* published by André Deutsch Ltd. 1990.

Hugo Williams for his poem '2001' © Hugo Williams 2002.

Will Wain on behalf of the John Wain Estate for 'This Above All is Precious and Remarkable' from *John Wain Poems 1949–1979* Macmillan, 1980.

David Higham Associates for 'On the Twelfth Day I Screamed' by David Daiches.

The Society of Authors as the Literary Representative of the Estate of Alfred Noyes for 'The Highwayman' by Alfred Noyes.

Faber and Faber Ltd, for 'As I Walked Out One Evening' by W.H. Auden from *The English Auden* Faber & Faber 1977.

New Directions Publishing Corporation, New York, for 'Your Laughter' by Pablo Neruda from *The Captains Verses*, translated by Donald D. Walsh, © 1972 by Pablo Neruda and Donald D. Walsh.

The Marvell Press, England and Australia, for 'Spring' by Philip Larkin from *The Less Deceived* published by The Marvell Press 1955.

Ben Okri for 'Grief' © Ben Okri 2002 all rights reserved.

Seamus Heaney for 'Chorus' from *The Cure at Troy* by Seamus Heaney, published by Faber and Faber Ltd 1990.

Dinah Livingstone for 'Revenge' by Luis Enrique Mejía Godoy, translated by Dinah Livingstone, from *Poets of the Nicaraguan Revolution*, published in bilingual text by Katabasis, London 1993.

The Orion Publishing Group Ltd. for 'The Bright Field' by R.S. Thomas from his *Collected Poems* published by J.M. Dent.

Adrian Mitchell for 'William Blake Says: Everything That Lives is Holy' © Adrian Mitchell 2001.

A.P. Watt Ltd. on behalf of The Royal Literary Fund for 'Oh God of Earth and Altar' by G.K. Chesterton from *Poems For All Purposes, Selected Poems of G.K. Chesterton* published by Pimlico 1994.

Saeed Jaffrey for 'Christ, the Prophet with the life-giving hand', by Ali Sardar Jafri, translated by Saeed Jaffrey.

Enitharmon Press for 'In the open' by Ruth Pitter, from *Ruth Pitter, Collected Poems* published by Enitharmon Press 1996.

Faber and Faber Ltd, for extract from 'Little Gidding' from *The Four Quartets, Collected Poems 1909–1962* by T.S. Eliot.

While every effort has been made to obtain permission from owners of copyright material reproduced herein, the publishers would like to apologise for any omissions and will be pleased to incorporate missing acknowledgements in any future editions.

INDEX OF CONTRIBUTORS

INDEX OF TITLES AND FIRST LINES

War Child is an International Relief and Development Agency, dedicated to providing immediate, effective and sustainable aid to children affected by war in order to build peace, resolve conflict and empower future generations.

War Child was founded in 1993 in response to the conflict in the former Yugoslavia. It has since expanded its work to conflicts worldwide, with an emphasis on Africa and Central Asia.

War Child strives to alleviate the suffering of children affected by war and to focus public attention on the plight of these children.

War Child is committed to the following principles. It will:

- Strive to uphold and promote the United Nation's Convention on the Rights of the Child.
- Work without regard for race, colour, sex, language, religion, sexuality, political or other opinion, national or social origin, property, birth or other status.
- Recognise the family as the natural environment for the growth and well-being of children.
- Work to support and develop already existing child welfare resources (e.g. parents, carers, teachers, local accountable organisations, etc).

War Child's ultimate goal is to enable children and young adults to exercise their rights and manage their own lives.

In addition to emergency relief and development projects War Child's work is centred on communications and education projects and the provision of safe, mine-free areas for children to play. These long-term projects are currently running in Rwanda, Sudan and the Balkans.

In response to the conflict in Afghanistan, War Child has deployed an emergency field bakery in the western city of Herat. The bakery is providing 25,000 displaced people a day with fresh bread, feeding the entire population of the nearby Shaidayee camp. War Child is now planning to expand its operation to cater for the longer-term needs of children and their families as the country recovers from the ravages of war.

War Child UK,
Ground Floor, Unit 3
5–7 Angler's Lane,
London
NW5 3DG
www.warchild.org.uk
tel. 020 7916 9276
fax 020 7916 9280